Let's Do It Right

A Journey from Exclusion to Inclusion

DEBASIS BHAUMIK

Editorial Project Management: Karen Rowe, www.karenrowe.com

Cover Design: Angela Hammersmith, hammersmithgraphics.com

Interior Layout: Ljiljana Pavkov

Printed in the United States

ISBN: 978-1-7770689-2-9 (paperback)
ISBN: 978-1-7770689-3-6 (digital)

To all humans who have accepted me unconditionally for who I am and included me in their life and space.

AUTHOR'S

NOTE

When necessary, I have used the terms "Black," "Brown" and other sometimes racially charged terms to designate people groups. My intent is not to offend. I believe diversity is beautiful and the word that describes all of us across the planet is "human."

Table of

Contents

Let's Do It Right

INTRODUCTION

In our quest for fairness, we have been asking the same question for decades: "How can we create equality?"

The journey for equality began long before the Emancipation Proclamation of the 19th century and the Civil Rights Act of the 20th century. It began with the early days of civilization and continues with the recent Black Lives Matter struggle. This journey takes us through every nation and every aspect of society, from homes and schools to churches and courtrooms, political campaigns to government offices, and from neighborhood parks to the streets in front of our houses. It has also become personal, dominating our social media and intimate conversations. And it has recently arrived in the corporate boardroom, prompting leaders to employ several new metrics and strategies. Meanwhile, inequality grants abundant opportunities to some while limiting others. That creates a struggle for power and radically different perceptions of reality.

As a corporate leader, I see the genuine efforts being made. Creating equality is an honorable endeavor, one that has been enthusiastically pursued. However, limited results cause me to wonder whether we are focused on the right things.

A quick google search reveals that Diversity, Equity, and Inclusion (DEI) are common topics in the business world. Many weigh in on the subject with their research, opinion, case studies, and recommendations. That is encouraging. Still, I am left with two critical questions. First, are DEI initiatives capable of engaging everyone? Second, are they sustainable and capable of delivering on their promises?

I believe we have veered off the best path to reach our destination.

To do it right, we must reach beyond the unattainable notion of equality. We are not all equal in talents or abilities and we never will be. However, we each need a fair chance to develop and contribute. To do it right, we must find a way to establish fair opportunities for each person.

In other words, we must do something humanity has thus far been unable to accomplish: establish *equity* in our organizations and society.

Roadmap

To understand why the quest for equity has been difficult and unrealized, we must take a journey through history, biology, and previous attempts. Therefore, Chapter 1 examines some history, some context, and some of my personal exposure to realities of diversity, inequality and inequity. Looking back, we recognize that the corporate drive for DEI is relatively new, while the drive toward equality has been active for centuries. Unfortunately, most of these drives have been narrowed with a short-term focus that did not stand the test of time. To do it right in the future, we must learn the lessons from history.

We continue the journey in Chapter 2 by examining the complex but often ignored understanding of biology, sociology, and psychology in human diversity. We are often too hard on ourselves, assuming all the issues with inclusions occur only because of our current social behaviors. Instead, we can shift from exclusion to inclusion with a broader understanding of how the sciences interact with the social aspects of our culture.

In Chapter 3, we pull over to ponder the possibilities of our journey at the overlook. Pausing, we take in the entire panorama of diversity, from the easy-to-see gender and skin color identifiers to the less visible but equally important range of beliefs, values, and abilities of the earth's population. Once we clarify our focus, we will see beyond the mirage of gender and skin color to accept reality: we live in a more diverse world than most of us recognize.

Chapter 4 continues with a necessary but unexpected detour. Titled "I Used to Be Majority," in these pages we examine how some efforts to include have inadvertently threatened the inclusion of the local majority. In our zeal for a solution, sometimes we have rushed to the remedy, overcompensating to bring about short-term solutions while ignoring the long-term inequities. To do it right, we must strike the delicate balance of including everyone—not just minorities.

 Chapter 5 turns the focus to equity as a core principle. Equity is far more than a handful of Key Performance Indicators—dimensions of diversity are too broad to list and be focused as KPIs—or a metric the EDI department employs in a certain set of activities. Instead, it should be a core principle that is applied in every aspect of a business and its action in society. Only when Equity is adopted as a core principle it is able to respect and celebrate diversity in a holistic manner. To do it right, we must appreciate each individual in the specific setting for the value they provide. Equity is a critical component of doing business well.

Chapter 6 steers us into the land of uncomfortable, strategic choices. Inclusion isn't an accident but a choice that we consciously make. The decision to become more inclusive is often threatening and leads us into unfamiliar and often terrifying territory. So, we take it slow, inching along, playing it safe. Inclusion without clarity and purpose can be paralyzing, but is playing it safe the best business practice? Almost nothing worthwhile can be achieved without an engaged team. This chapter offers a strategy to overcome employee disengagement: combine psychological safety with inclusion to drive engagement and high-performance outcomes.

We forge ahead in Chapter 7, where I introduce the 2x2 Awareness and Acceptance framework. This was created based on my real-life experience while working in multiple geographies, through formal and informal cross-industry conversations with corporate leaders. Here, I explain the purpose and definition of the 2x2 framework, which helps individuals and organizations progress along spectrums of awareness and acceptance to finally achieve belief.

Implementation of most framework starts with an assessment. In Chapter 8, I offer a recommendation and guidance questionnaire to help you assess your organizational or individual position on the acceptance-to-belief spectrum depicted by the 2x2 framework. Assessing this point in the journey is important to baseline EDI. It allows us to actually measure progress.

Chapter 9 requires that we continue our journey with purposeful action. Actions focused on awareness and acceptance will increase inclusion. That is what helps us do inclusion right.

The final stop on our journey is persistence: a complex problem that will not be solved immediately. Old habits die hard, and ancient prejudices are deeply rooted. Making the change to inclusion may feel like moving a mountain. After all, the human race has been working on these problems from the beginning of civilization, and it will take more time, tremendous effort, and intentional thoughtfulness to make such a monumental change. Fear not. Equity is not a lost cause, and your efforts are valuable. Do not overlook the opportunity to build a future pipeline, starting with education at an early age and patiently but persistently changing the perspective.

In the end, the journey is worth the effort. Join me on this voyage so we can all do it right. In the end, we will all benefit.

CHAPTER 1:

SOME HISTORY, SOME CONTEXT, and ME

My first memory of diversity and inequality, or maybe my sense of "wrong," happened on a hot and humid Sunday in Kolkata, India, when I was around seven years old.

Back then, I lived with my parents and sister in a very humble portion of the main floor of a rented two-story house. Our entire living space measured about fifteen feet by thirteen feet. This included everything except the bathrooms, which were detached from the house. On that Sunday, my mother was trying to get lunch prepared at one end of the space on her earthen oven, fueled by coal and cow dung cakes. My baby sister and I were playing with some toys at the other end. My father was out and about, taking care of some chores. We heard a knock, which was normal for a house on the main street with an accessible front door. We were not allowed to open the door as kids, but I stood on the window sill and peeped outside. I saw a lady in a torn Sari with a skinny, naked boy wearing the tiniest, torn shorts. My mom, not willing to be interrupted, called out, "Sorry, we can't help now. We are very busy. Come another time."

I continued to watch, and for a moment my eyes connected with the little boy's. I then watched as the mother and son pair continued on to knock at the next house.

The boy was around my age, and I felt an unusual, strong connection with him, as if I could see myself in his place. Even after all these years, I have never been able to shake the feeling. The image of an almost naked little boy wandering the streets with his mother, begging for scraps, had become forever imprinted on my mind. Within minutes, I was unable to control my emotions and broke into tears. "We have to help this kid," I repeated, over and over. "I want to give him one of my toy cars." Maybe I thought toy was more important than food for him.

My parents tried everything they could think of to distract me, but nothing worked. After a while, they realized I would not stop unless they took action and helped the pair who had come begging at our door. My dad was my childhood hero; he would do anything for me. I somehow had faith that something would happen when he decided to act. He went out to search the unpredictable lanes of our old Kolkata neighborhood in an attempt track them down. Finally, he returned with them and gave them a plate of rice and lentils. They ate it all very quickly while sitting at our doorstep, and I gave the boy my little white car with a recoil spring. I remember that toy car more vividly than the real cars I have owned since.

Looking back, it was not skin color or gender at birth that arrested my attention—it was the massive financial and social diversity on display that shocked me. As far as I can remember, that was the first time I became aware of different social strata.

Gendered Expectations

As I grew older, more pictures painted themselves in my head. I observed that most of my aunts in India stayed at home to raise kids and make lunch. Moms might have been the final decision makers in each household, but they rarely worked outside of the home. Instead, their male counterparts went out to become breadwinners, taking care of grocery buying and most outdoor chores. My home was no different.

However, there were exceptions. A few of my aunts were gainfully employed outside the house, and so were the mothers of some of my friends. There was a very limited set of jobs available to them that mostly followed general ideas about "women's work." Many of them were school or college teachers. Very few of them were in manufacturing, sales or office type jobs. Generally speaking, their jobs hardly ever required overnight travel for work.

I grew up with the distinct feeling that I actually enjoyed my time and conversation with the aunts who worked outside the home more than others. It was an overgeneralized observation in my mind: they were a notch more superior than the other lovely ladies in my life who, whether by choice or lack of options, stayed home.

My mom fell into that category. She stayed at home for most of her life. Like me, she also looked up to her sister, who was a high school teacher. Mom valued that sister's opinion more than my other aunts.'

I had other brushes with gendered expectations in my youth. I went to a co-ed school. Though that is very normal today, most of the schools in the India of my youth were either for boys or girls. For example, my wife, brother-in-law, and sister-in-law all went to better catholic schools that were either a boys' school *or* a girls' school. However, from age three I always was in an environment where we played, studied, and did mischief together, and I did not see any differences in the life experiences of my friends who happened to be girls.

But today, while writing this book, something occurred to me. I started thinking about my sister in our childhood. Through my eyes, we were treated the same by our parents and relatives. That was my understanding, and it is mostly true. But my sister's experience included something very different from mine.

My unstructured play hours were the most precious part of the day for me. I loved sports and being outdoors with friends from my community. We "called" each other by knocking on doors and then decided on the fly whether the day would be spent playing soccer (we called it "football"), cricket, or just goofing around and riding bikes. One thing was constant every day of the year: we enjoyed two to three hours of play time at a local park or field with friends. Given all that time, I turned out to be a decent self-taught cricket and soccer player.

Meanwhile, what did my sister do during those hours? I had never bothered to think about it before, so I did not know. That was strange because I knew everything she did during the rest of the day. Later I learned that she stayed home with my mom, played with her dolls, or with the little girl next door.

I know my sister enjoyed playing cricket, soccer, and riding her bike. Why didn't I take her with me? Why didn't she say something? Why didn't she make a big deal of it? I decided to call her up and ask.

"I actually did make a big deal few times," she said, "but always heard the same 'no.' Soon, 'separate guidance for girls' just became normal for me."

My sister and I are very close, so close that I hired her as my first programmer in my startup. She earned a Master of Computer Sciences degree and has a physics background; she is a better programmer and more advanced in STEM than me. She definitely broke through that ceiling in many ways.

But while answering my question she laughed a bit, and then became quiet. A bit of silence followed. I figured that I reminded her of some things in her life which she did not cherish or enjoy. I also felt ashamed that I'd never thought to ask until now.

The reason I am talking about my experience and observation of females in my life is because I think it shows how unconscious biases take root in us and guide our thoughts. Whether we realize it or not, the patterns that shape our society imprint themselves in our minds from childhood, and they form our beliefs and biases. Becoming conscious of them is a first step. We will talk about this more later.

Vortex of Poverty

When I was in middle school, a never-before seen phenomena was introduced: a cafeteria where students and teachers could buy hot lunches and snacks. It was one the most amazing things, my younger self thought – almost life-changing! I was always given one piece of a sweet cube (*chamcham*) and two crackers for my lunch every day, which my dad bought the night before

As I grew and started playing sports, I was famished by the second half of the school day. But by then I knew that the lunch budget my parents had for each of us was very limited; I would make it more difficult for them if I asked for more. To this day I have no clue if my dad even had lunch, or if he mostly went without. My guess is it was probably the latter. Around that period my mom suddenly got religious and started following several weekly rituals which all included fasting. I am also not sure whether that choice was truly a religious inclination or something else. I chose not to ask her anything that could take away the pride she has about raising us well.

Perhaps it's no wonder the school cafeteria had more attraction to me at that time than any Michelin rated restaurants in the best locations of the world now. Its existence turned me into a version of the boy with the tiny shorts I'd seen through the front window of our family rooms. I watched as most kids ate and had fun buying from cafeteria, but I did not have cash to do the same. One day a girl I knew, let's call her Suzy, offered me half of a fish chop. It was—and still is—the most amazing thing I ever ate. It was partly the cooking, partly my long wait to taste something from that cafeteria.

My dad's ability to prioritize was amazing; he had immense clarity around what was within bounds and what was out of bounds for us.

He was also equally clear about his means and priorities regarding the family finances and expenses; growing up, he made our financial status abundantly clear. I knew beyond a shadow of doubt that we belonged to the lower side of the spectrum.

As I grew older, I started recognizing the sliding scale of economic diversity. Again I experienced a sense of helplessness, similar yet quite different to the feelings I had when the little boy and his mom showed up at our door for food.

While I was admittedly oblivious to the differences my sister lived through, by high school I had become a very careful observer of the economic diversity which lead to exclusion and inequality. Heading into high school, the biggest diversity and discomfort I was aware of was that a person's financial class came as a result of their social lifestyle. It was perfectly clear in my head. I knew I had to have a plan to address it, and I did: work hard, start earning soon, and help my immediate circle first. It was the only way I saw to escape the vortex of poverty and achieve some means of equality.

I did not know the term equity at that time. Instead, *equality* felt like the missing piece. By age sixteen, I started earning money by tutoring other students in Mathematics and Science. Little by little, I earned enough tax-free cash to get the first wired telephone, refrigerator, and music player for my family—and, most importantly, the first pair of jeans for my sister. I chose not to standardize my tutoring fees. I taught some students for free, some for high fees, and some in the middle. It was my first response to social inequity.

At that time, I also started teaching and training underprivileged kids who were part of the child labor workforce. To me, education is the best gift because it is an opportunity to stretch our minds every day. I enjoyed those days of teaching.

During this journey of volunteer teaching, I met a few other well-read young adults who were also actively volunteering. They impressed me with their knowledge and their personal and political perspectives. From them I first heard the word *comrade*. They started loaning me books and taking me to meetings, where they discussed what I interpreted as *the journey to the end of inequality*. It was a romantic experience; I was fascinated with what I was learning. I began writing poetry and reading whatever I could get my hands on.

Inequality Through the Ages

Gradually, it became clear to me that I was not the first person to be bothered by inequality. Throughout the ages—and especially in the last three centuries—many attempts have been made to create equality. In ancient Greece, Plato and other thought leaders imagined an island where money had been abolished, and people lived and worked in a commune.[1] Theirs were some of the first iterations of utopia, though they did not use that word. Many, many efforts would follow, but efforts to establish utopian societies were mostly futile. Robert Owen, a Welsch industrialist, planted several utopian communities in the United States to create a "radically equal society." However, none survived. As I read of each failure, I wondered if equality could be contrary to human nature—and, therefore, impossible.

Still, cries for equality from the voices of leaders in various disciplines have resonated throughout history. Swiss theologian and critic Alexandre Vinet coined the term "socialism" in 1830 as the polar opposite of individualism.[2] Count Henri de Saint-Simon was fascinated by science and technology as a means of balancing the inequities of capitalism. He argued for a society where everyone was rewarded for their abilities and contributions. This meritocratic society countered the caste and class system, in which people were rewarded for their family lineage.[3] Enter David Ricardo, working in the field of economics. He questioned whether the factors of profit, interest, and rent should be considered deductions from the exchange value.[4] Then came Karl Marx and his 1848 work "The Communist Manifesto." Marx and his collaborator, Friedrich Engels, argue: "True Scientific Socialism could be established only after a revolutionary class struggle with workers emerging on top." Marx was not interested in utopian blueprints but believed in actual mass movements.

---

[1] Dailyhistory.org.

[2] Cort, John C. "Christian socialism." Orbis Books, New York, 1988. pp. 355.

[3] Alan Ryan. *On Politics*. Book II. 2012. pp. 647–651.

[4] Ricardo, David. *Principles of Political Economy and Taxation* (1817).

Although these and other efforts were meant to improve life for the masses, they often left people in a worse state. The Revolution of 1917 that swelled into communist Soviet Union would be shattered by 1991. Like Robert Owens' utopian societies, these efforts for equality were torn down; the Berlin Wall was toppled by the very labor unions and citizens communism was designed to protect.

As I continued my reading and learning, I started to doubt that inequality could be corrected by attempting utopias. Instead, I became more convinced of the necessity for a happy medium between the extremes of communes and capitalism. The evidence before me was plain: the age-old battle between self-sufficiency and equality was not only real, it had been raging for centuries. But was our quest for equality focused on guaranteeing equal results or the equality of opportunity?

Denmark, Finland, Sweden, and Norway seem to have found a balance. These Nordic countries, which consistently rank near the top of the world in happiness and human development, have highly organized labor markets, universal welfare states, and relatively high levels of public ownership of capital. Given their success, we should look closer. Does their system model the balance we are all looking for?

Or, is equal representation the answer? Should we follow the idea of some leaders, who believed a percentage of corporate board seats should be reserved for a company's workers? Does the U.S. need a universal basic income? Should college student loans be forgiven? Should college be tuition-free for all?

In an honest effort to answer these policy questions, perhaps we need to consider one very potent question: what is the reality of equality?

The Reality of Equality

The word "equality" sounds interesting and righteous, with a romantic edge. Who can resist the enticing concepts of *equal justice* and *equal representation*? Equality looks bold in print and sounds provocative in a public speech, but is it merely a mirage? How real is it? How realistic should it be? What relevance should it have in our lives?

Let's look at nature. The solar system is not equal. The planets are not equal in size, are not the same distance from the sun, and do not have the same climates. Imagine Mercury, Earth, and Jupiter in the same sun orbit. Imagine Mars complaining because it doesn't have as many rings as Saturn. Imagine Uranus complaining because it is on the outer edge. Then imagine what poor old Pluto would say after being removed from the list. To establish equality, do we remove the rings from Saturn, the moons from Jupiter, or life on Earth?

Then examine the flowers. Should they all be equal in shape, size, and color? Should everyone have the same flowers of the same quality in their garden? If so, does that mean everyone has an equal amount of the same noxious weeds?

We admire the mountains because they stand in dramatic fashion to the plains. We notice the gorgeous sunsets as they dramatically paint the sky. They stand out against the uniformity of grey, overcast ones.

Nature has never displayed anything equally, and in this we find beauty. Uniqueness draws attention and diversity brings texture.

The same is true for the human world. Some strains of Communism argue that when uniformity is mandated, everyone earns the same income and lives in the same type of home—every child should even have the same toys. Sometimes these ideologies dictate how many children a couple can have. Unfortunately, that brand of "equality" creates a grey landscape devoid of colors. However generous the word equality might sound, it is not practical to foist complete uniformity upon everyone.

Suppose a school gives equal-sized bicycles to all students. While that sounds "fair," let's consider the reality. Is every child in that school the same height and weight? Do they all have the same ability or desire to handle the same bike?

I saw this happen in real life. A government program in South Asia delivered identical bikes to every child in a high school, despite the fact that girls were expected to wear flowing Saris to school.

Imagine trying to pedal a bike while wearing a socially mandated garment that could easily get caught in the gears and cause an accident. Worse, two kids in the school were differently abled; it was not even an option for them to ride the same bikes as everyone else.

Providing uniformity is often not practical, so how can we possibly mandate equality? The answer is that we cannot. Equality in everything is not realistic. That is not the way of nature.

Perhaps we should ask ourselves if we even *want* equality. Imagine staring at equal landscapes, experiencing "seasons" with equal characteristics year in and year out, and living in cities with houses of equal heights and colors. Now imagine that everyone does the same job at the same time in the same way.

Also, imagine everyone making the same amount of money and living in the same city in the same climate. Not only is that boring, it is also unrealistic. We cannot conceive of such a world.

Equality is an enticing concept, but it is just that. A concept.

Equality is also a powerful moral and political *ideal* that has inspired and guided human society for centuries. It is implicit in most faiths and religions, which proclaim all human beings to be the creation of God. As a political ideal, the concept of equality invokes the idea that all human beings have equal worth regardless of their color, gender, race, or nationality. It maintains that human beings deserve equal consideration and respect because of their common humanity. Socialists have always favored the word equality for its insistence on a more equal distribution of wealth and income within society. This is in sharp contrast to those who favor equality of opportunity, not just wealth.

Equality vs Equity

Historically, *equality* has been a political term, a rallying cry in the struggle against states and social institutions that uphold inequalities of rank, wealth, status, or privilege among people. In the 18th century, French revolutionaries used the slogan "Liberty, Equality, and Fraternity" to revolt against the landed feudal aristocracy and the monarchy. The demand for equality was also raised during anti-colonial liberation struggles in Asia and Africa during the 20th century. It continues to be raised by struggling groups such as the Dalits (considered lower in the caste system) of India, who feel marginalized even today.

The definition of equality shifts depending on the focus of the struggle. Marxists and socialists feel that economic inequality supports other forms of social inequality, such as differences of rank or privilege. To them, tackling inequality demands going beyond providing equal opportunities to ensure public control over essential resources and forms of property. Meanwhile, capitalist societies uphold the principle of competition as the most efficient and fair way of distributing resources and rewards in society. They believe that while states may have to intervene to try and ensure a minimum standard of living and equal opportunities for all, this cannot by itself bring equality and justice to society. Competition between people in free and fair conditions is considered the most just and efficient way of distributing rewards in society. Every child is allowed to pursue their dreams. Every worker has the opportunity to develop their talents and be considered for the best jobs.

This is why the term *equality* is itself the source of confusion and should be changed. Instead, we need to consider using *equality of opportunity*.

Undoubtedly, many will say, "that's what I meant," but the distinction is, at best, implied. Meanwhile, the unrealistic notion of *equality of results* is also implied, especially for the have-nots. The two notions of 'equality of results' and 'equality of opportunity' are different. However, striving for either type of equality requires sacrifice from someone else. Those in power, the *haves*, must allow others, the *have-nots*, to develop their abilities and be allowed to compete on a level playing field. That is where the challenge comes. Who wants to give up any privilege they have inherited or earned? Somewhere along the journey of history, the elite and powerful have gained an advantage. They will claim they earned it, but as we examine the situation closely, there are institutional, social, and political advantages they enjoy but did not earn. Balancing that inequality of opportunity will create considerable tension. Why would those in power want to give it up when they believe they have earned it or deserve it? Why would they demand a level playing field for those not in power that could threaten their advantage?

Equality

The terms equality,[5] equal, and equally signify a qualitative relationship. Equality (or equal) signifies correspondence between a group of different objects, persons, processes, or circumstances that have the same qualities in at least one respect but not all respects.

Too often, we see equal as *identical*.

However, judgments of equality presume a difference between the things being compared. According to this definition, the notion of *complete* or *absolute* equality is problematic as it violates the presumption of a difference. Equality and equal are incomplete predicates that necessarily generate one question: equal in what respect? Two non-identical objects are never completely equal; they are different, at least in their spatiotemporal location. If things do not differ, they should not be called equal but rather, more precisely, identical, such as the morning and the evening star.

In fact, equality consists of a three-way relation between several objects and qualities. Say two objects, A and B, are equal in a certain respect if, in that respect, they fall under the same general term. Equality then signifies the relationship between the objects being compared. Every comparison presumes a tertium, or third element created from a combination of two known elements. In that synergistic perspective, equality refers to a common sharing of this comparison-determining attribute. Yes, equality is achieved through sharing. But to understand what we achieve from this triangular experiment is something that needs to be specified in each

---

[5] Greek *isotes*; Latin *aequitas, aequalitas*; French *égalité*; German *Gleichheit*.

case.[6] Determining equality depends on the descriptive or norma-
tive moral standard we employ. Now, consider that we will measure
equality differently depending on what standard we employ.[7] The
difference between a general concept and different specific con-
ceptions of equality may explain why some people claim equality
has no unified meaning – or is even devoid of meaning.[8], [9]

For this reason, it helps to think of the idea of equality or inequality in
the context of social justice, not as a single principle but as a complex group of principles forming the basic core of today's egalitar-
ianism. Different principles yield different answers. In any historical
context, it is clear that no single notion of equality can sweep the
field. Take, for example, the "Great Britain's Equality and Human
Rights Commission of Great Britain 2018" report. Great Britain tried
to play fair and not equal. They took over six areas of everyday life
and attempted to improve the next generation's opportunities in an
environment created to be 'just and fair,' but avoids the term 'equal.'
As per the report, three in ten children live in poverty, and more than
half of all children from Black African, Pakistani, and Bangladeshi
households live in poverty. Only 12 percent of Gypsy, Roma, and
Traveler children achieve a good level of secondary school attainment, compared with 64 percent of White British children.

Equity

As my formative years stretched into adulthood, I became increasingly aware that equity is a more relevant concept than equality.

It has been proven that no two people are the same, and therefore
no two needs are the same. Even our need for equal opportunity is
not the same. Equity recognizes the difference between the starting
point and creating a level playing field. It aims at making opportunities and circumstances similar for all. Because each person has

---

[6] Westen 1990, p. 10.

[7] Temkin, 1986, 1993, 2009.

[8] Rawls 1971, p. 21 f.

[9] Rae 1981, p. 127 f., 132 f.

different circumstances, resources need to be allocated so that those with fewer opportunities get more, so they can come on par with those who have more.

Changing our language shifts our perspective. Equity is about creating an environment where certain rules apply to certain people in specific circumstances. To say some rules are applicable for those under nineteen years old, while others are relevant for those under twenty years old understands the equity involved. In the same way, there are different rules for competing in the Olympics than there are for competing in the Paralympics. Those rules are equitable but not equal. Equity allows people living under similar circumstances better opportunities so that they are given the possibility to perform and outperform each other.

Equity is prudent because it accepts the reality of diversity. This applies to political and corporate structures. DEI contains the letter E, which stands for equity and refers to the policies that support diversity and inclusion in the company. It is about recognizing that everyone is unique and properly accommodating their needs. One can discover tangible, real-world solutions by acknowledging the company's structural imbalances. Equity-first businesses go through a consistent process of redressing the balance of opportunity. It's a matter of recognizing that certain groups are subject to advantages and disadvantages that manifest in a variety of ways, such as gender pay gaps or biased onboarding practices, and taking direct, sustained action.

Equality vs. Equity in the Workplace

Equality in the workplace assumes all employees are the same and treats them as such. While this sounds inclusive, it is incredibly open to bias and ignores demographic-specific needs. Equity, on the other hand, recognizes that we are all different and concludes that our differences make each of us great. Rather than blanket policies, equity-led businesses consider individual needs while rebalancing structures to account for disadvantages faced by minority groups. In contrast, a socialistic approach seeks identical policies, procedures, and performance from various abilities and interests. For that reason, we shift from the focus on equality to emphasize equity.

The challenge comes when companies strive for workplace equality (treating everyone equally, without considering diversity). They often do not factor in the need for equity. The entire workforce comes under the same blanket of rules, privileges, and employee experience design without consideration for unique, demographic, or diversity-related needs. This may lead to an unfair work environment.

Equity, on the other hand, helps identify specific needs and requirements informed by demographic traits such as ethnicity, nationality, age, gender, and ability. It then tries to address the differing needs of each group by bridging the gap between minority and majority groups. This makes equity central to the genuine empowerment of minority groups (and not just a theoretical possibility).

Equity can be as simple as dining options. Amelia Ransom, senior director of engagement and diversity at Avalara, a company that provides automated tax software, says, "Equity provides vegan and vegetarian options along with the meat meal so that everybody has something they can eat. To have equity in your organization, there needs to be an understanding of what each person needs and wants to be successful in the workplace."

It can also be as complex as self-worth and human rights. In recent years, thousands took to the streets in the summer of 2020 to ask the world a compelling question: *do we matter?* After centuries of slavery, neglect, and abuse, those who have been marginalized and dismissed demanded an answer.

Black Lives Matter and Workplace Equity

The most recent moment in our journey to do it right occurred during the 2020 mass protests and riots across the United States. The Covid-19 virus had effectively sequestered the world; just as we were reemerging from quarantine, three white police officers in a northern city violated police protocol. Once again, a Black man had died at the hands of a White police officer.

George Floyd's was yet another senseless death. But this time, it wasn't in a former slave state like Alabama, Georgia, or South Carolina, but in Minneapolis, the capital of a state known for "Minnesota Nice." The injustice ignited pent-up frustration and the peaceful streets exploded. Most intense and prolonged in Portland, Oregon and Seattle, Washington, the protests lingered in cities not necessarily known for their large black populations. With chants of "Black Lives Matter," the excluded raised their voices, focusing attention on the latest police injustice. With little else to report, the media couldn't escape the message: *you will pay attention, and this inequity must end now*. The world and, more importantly, politicians could no longer ignore this persistent problem.

Neither could corporate America.

Diversity, equity, and inclusion discussions were already making the rounds in boardrooms and on investor calls before 2020. However, the Black Lives Matter movement became a global catalyst for change inside those same corporate boardrooms. Sensing the urgency, several major corporate organizations pledged a $50 billion-dollar investment (about $150 per person in the US) to remove systemic racism. The list included many large brands like Citi, IBM, Nike, JP Morgan Chase, and Capital One.

But while the Black Lives Matter pendulum finally began to swing in the direction of equity, other inequities surfaced. Attacks against Asians increased as they were unfairly blamed for the Coronavirus outbreak and the pandemic. Meanwhile, reports of other hate acts surfaced throughout the United States and the globe, even across caste- and religion-based divides in countries like India.

Although the stories were rife with negativity, they brought awareness to the masses. With that came an intense resolve to repair what had been broken for so long. Years of promises were finally fulfilled as governmental and corporate policies began to change. I personally witnessed several corporate boards recognize their responsibility by establishing and improving their DEI strategy. Racism was no longer just a government issue.

Steps Toward Equity

Unfortunately, this is no fairy tale in which everyone lives happily ever after. In June 2021, hundreds of unmarked graves were discovered on the grounds of state-run boarding schools for Indigenous children in Canada that were open between 1863 and 1998. Whispers and rumors persisted until the first grave was discovered. Then public outrage increased with the discovery of each additional grave, which soon numbered more than 6,000. As the father of an eight-year-old, my heart cried for all those innocent kids and their families. As a Canadian citizen, my civic pride was shattered. How could this happen?

That is when I decided to author this book. I began by reading about indigenous history when a fellow board member gifted me with a copy of *Dancing with a Ghost: Exploring an Aboriginal Reality*.[10] But as I read and followed the DEI strategies of large organizations, I became more bewildered about how to proceed on our shared journey to equity.

As corporate citizens and members of the human race, we must ask poignant questions. Is it about "Black Lives Matter" or "Asian Lives Matter?" Do our efforts also include acceptance of people of all sexual orientations, welcoming people of all abilities, tolerance for all religions, and acceptance of all classes and status? More generally, what is the scope of equity, and what does it look like in practice and across diverse global populations? We have traveled this road for our entire existence on planet earth, but seem to have wandered in circles. Are we finally to a point where we can ask the tough questions and, even more importantly, find the solution?

In the global age, racism and inequity are world issues that affect us all. Never before have we been so connected through technology, freedom of movement, and awareness. Someone else's injustice quickly appears on my personal phone. Unlike in the past, you and I can no longer hide from the injustice to others.

---

[10] Rupert Ross, 1992.

CONCLUSION

In our journey to balance inequality, we considered the struggle to create equilibrium between the haves and the have-nots. Over the centuries, leaders have sought to create utopian societies where everyone enjoyed equal benefits. However well-intentioned, those efforts were not sustainable. Whether in Owen's utopian communities in the United States or Marx's communistic U.S.S.R., achieving this idea proved unrealistic. Instead, this book dismisses the word equality in favor of a more realistic approach defined as equity.

KEY TAKEAWAYS

- Several attempts have been made to establish equality within cultures. Socialism once served a purpose in this world, but worldwide it has been largely rejected over time.
- If everything in nature was equal, we might reach a stalemate where nothing is interesting or valuable.
- Equity is an effort to make opportunities and circumstances similar for most.
- Equity recognizes that each person has different circumstances and allocates resources needed to reach an environment of equal opportunity.

CHAPTER 2:

BIOLOGY, SOCIOLOGY and PSYCHOLOGY OF HuMAN DIVERSITY

Having explored a short history of human society's reaction to inequity through the centuries, and my personal exposure to the same, we now focus on understanding the biological, psychological, and social drivers for aspects of diversity: race, gender, and class. This chapter will hopefully open our thinking around why such diversities exist among humans. It's time to celebrate diversities and embrace equity for a new world?

DIVERSITY

Pele and Me

When I was just a preschooler, my avid soccer fan father took me to a very large stadium. He wanted me to watch the man he called "the God of Soccer."

Right away I noticed something shocking: Pele was unlike most idols or gods I was familiar with. He had darker skin and was quite a bit larger than most of the adults I was used to seeing around me.

"Why does Pele have a different skin color than mine?" I asked my dad.

Dad would usually take time to answer most of my questions, but not that day. He was too absorbed Pele's playing; he was soaking in the presence of his "god." Finally, he said, "He has African origins and he takes after his parents."

I did not understand, but I imagined that his parents must look like him. I had often heard adults making small talk about whether a kid took after their mom or dad, and I even heard folks talking about my looks in the same way. But why did Pele's parents look different than my parents or my grandparents? That question went unanswered, and might have even been one I didn't know how to ask.

Since then, I have observed that an increasing number of international soccer players came to Kolkata to play in club soccer. Most of them were university students, originally from Nigeria, and they were very tall. Our local players hardly reached the Nigerians' shoulders. It was very interesting to see that diversity, color, and size in action in a local soccer team.

The quest to understand why we look different has been in me since then. I liked the reasoning that said the parents' looks were passed down to their kids, because I could see the physical resemblances for myself. That kind of evidence was satisfying to my kid brain.

But it was in later years, over an extended period spent studying Darwin's survival of the fittest and concepts of evolution in school, that I began to form a story about how nature could have shaped some of the diversities I saw every day. I did not know the word diversity then. Instead, I referred to them as differences.

Human Evolution and Darwin

The evolution of modern humans was a complex process involving major changes in levels of diversity through time. The fossils and stone tools that record the spatial distribution of our species form the backbone of our evolutionary history. That knowledge allows us to explore the different cultural and biological processes that shaped the evolution of different populations in the face of major climate, social, and political changes. Those processes created complex changes with similarities and differences that were accelerated by sharp demographic and geographical fluctuations.

The result is an evolution.

Because of that evolution, we look and behave very differently than our ancient ancestors.

Our understanding of human diversity reflects a vast amount of missing information from the 200,000-year-old history of humans. While we have gained considerable knowledge, much is yet to be discovered, understood, and applied.

For example, we have inadequately mapped African origin and have limited knowledge about how we have been shaped by its major geographical and demographic expansions. That is especially true regarding a period that occurred approximately 150,000 years ago, when human populations dispersed across Africa and, eventually, into Eurasia. This expansive migration reveals an important insight for understanding human diversity evolution mechanisms: it is not the same throughout the world. Nor does it have universal triggers.

Instead, modern-day diversity was the result of several macro and micro-evolutionary processes. As populations dispersed across Africa, Asia, and Europe, they encountered various ecological conditions that demanded adaptation. Each clan, determined to survive, formed a slightly different society with various economic, social, and cultural practices. Those living in the desert developed differently than those living in the mountains. Depending upon their environment and abilities, humans adapted and diversified at different paces.

However, not all populations survived. When small groups became extinct, surviving groups expanded into the areas left vacant. Meanwhile, regardless of location, populations expanded and evolved at different paces. Whether they succeeded appears to depend upon each population's distance from other societies. The farther a given society's remove from the larger concentration, the slower its growth.

We see this today, in the way urban centers are more progressive than remote, rural areas. Time can stand still in one area, while inter-action with a diverse population promotes the kind of change that we call *progress*. This evolutionary process results in periods of rapid population growth for some groups and the extinction of others. Since the dawn of time, it has served as a filter, through which only certain traits and characteristics survive.

A comprehensive overview of human evolution is outside the scope of this book, but it is still helpful to make ourselves aware of rele-vant scientific context. As biologist Robert Trivers explains, removing science simply leaves opinion—in the form of words with magical powers to create bias—and leads to time wasted arguing, instead of synthesizing social and physical anthropology. If we ignore the biology of evolution that created our differences, we will not see dis-cussions of inclusion beyond the level of single, isolated societies.[11]

Understanding and appreciating diversity's biological factors allows us to appreciate the way certain traits allow individuals to adapt to their environments, helping them survive threats and produce off-spring that will inherit their traits and continue to adapt. Meanwhile, individuals with less adaptive traits will less frequently survive or reproduce. Survival of the fittest decides which forms will survive in the long run. Over time, the traits that allow a species to survive and reproduce will become more frequent in the population, and the population will change or evolve accordingly. Through natural selection, as Darwin suggested, diverse life forms could thus arise from a common ancestor.

From this perspective, our biological diversity and similarity can be traced through human migration across the earth. That migration has

---

[11] *The Folly of Fools: The Logic of Deceit and Self-Deception in Human Life*. Basic Books, 2011.

led to a continual evolution where divergent groups connected and reproduced, merging traits with the strongest surviving members.

For example, primitive humans that evolved through the millennia gave rise to the modern human form. Notice how humans have changed throughout history. The first humans, known as *Homo habilis*, or "Handy Man," lived 2.4 million to 1.4 million years ago in Eastern and Southern Africa. Then came *Homo rudolfensis*, who lived in Eastern Africa 1.9 million to 1.8 million years ago. The third category, known as *Homo erectus*, or the 'Upright Man' migrated from Southern Africa to modern-day China and Asia, living between 1.89 million to 110,000 years ago. Recently, scientists discovered modern human teeth that date to approximately 80 ka in China, which indicates early migration beyond western Asia and establishes the first modern human populations in eastern and presumably southeastern Asia prior to the main dispersal events that took place 20,000 to 30 000 years later. Recent genetic evidence shows that the Altai Neanderthals carry genetic signatures from two different populations: Eurasia, and another group that has become extinct.[12] Each of these eras offered different human characteristics and development.

RACE
Nelson Mandela and My Card

Pele was not my only brush with diversity as a child, of course. In school, I learned about Nelson Mandela. I had learned about Gandhi and others who were not alive in my lifetime there too, from history books. But Mandela was different. He was alive. I thought I could connect with him by sending wishes in a large card we created for him in our school.

Photos and video of Mandela gave me the opportunity to see someone else who looked like Pele. To me, something very wrong was happening to him and his followers because he was Black. Such

---

[12] History.com.

was my zeal for his plight that I remember putting a lot of thought into a four-line poem I composed and wrote for the card. It was sensational; it was different. It was the feeling of youth contributing towards a revolution in Mandela's nation's journey towards right. I read about India's struggle for revolution for independence in history. It felt like being part of history in making.

I still have no idea what happened to the card and letters our school collected from all of us. But later on, when Mandela was released from prison, I felt I had contributed to undoing the great wrong he had experienced. Through that experience, I had also been introduced to the word "racism" for the first time.

Race

There is much more to race and class than a social construct. By the end of the 16th century, the word "race" had entered the English language. It was originally used loosely, to refer to people of common descent who could be identified by their shared culture and ties to a geographic place. Increasing contact with people of Africa and Asia led to distinctions based on differences in appearance. In popular usage, European whites began to group races based on skin color—white and Black, for example, among others.

In the eighteenth century, science got involved. Naturalists Carl Linnaeus and Johann Blumenbach proposed formal groupings of populations into races based on distinctive morphological features. By the middle of the nineteenth century, scholars had decided that the different races were not only cosmetically and morphologically distinctive but also had different personalities and intellectual characteristics. They argued that the differences amounted to a racial hierarchy, with whites on top and blacks at the bottom. These so-called scientific writings occurred in the context of the Europeans' colonization of the New World. In South and North America alike, the incomers displaced and almost eradicated indigenous populations who already occupied the land. They enslaved and imported Black Africans and incorporated slavery into their social systems.

As I learned about the history, I was struck by the inherent *wrong-ness* of slavery. Combined with what I knew about world leaders like Nelson Mandela, Abraham Lincoln, and Gandhi, I began to explore what differences between humans were, in fact, "real."

As I dug further, it became obvious to me that racism is not the exclusive domain of the white European/American man. Racism has raged throughout the Asian culture as well. To see it requires looking no farther than a common theme: those in power tend to exclude those who are not of the same race, class, or gender.

Among scholars, however, the opening of the twentieth century saw a scientific backlash against the idea of racial hierarchies and against the idea of race itself. One of the most prominent spokesmen was Franz Boas (July 9, 1858 – December 21, 1942), a pioneering anthropologist and a fierce opponent of what he called "scientific racism."[13] Boas made two important propositions. First, that the genetic differences among human populations are insignificant. Second, that humans left Africa too recently for important differences to have evolved. Boas' work became foundational to later writings about race, including work by geneticist Richard Lewontin and paleontologist Stephen Jay Gould.[14]

In 1972, Lewontin also analyzed genetic diversity among different races with the tools available at the time and found that less than 15 percent of all genetic diversity is accounted for by differences among groups.[15] He says:

It is clear that our perception of relatively large differences between human races and subgroups, as compared to the variation within these groups, is indeed a biased perception and that, based on randomly chosen genetic differences, human races and populations are remarkably similar to each other, with the largest part by far of human variation being accounted for by the differences

---

[13] Biography.com.

[14] For instance, see their article, "The Spandrels of San Marco and the Panglossian Paradigm: A Critique of the Adaptationist Programme."

[15] See "The Apportionment of Human Diversity."

between individuals. Human racial classification is of no social value and is positively destructive of social and human relations. Since such racial classification is now seen to be of virtually no genetic or taxonomic significance either, no justification can be offered for its continuance.

The division of humans into modern "racial" groups is a product of our recent history. In the end, there is hardly any genetic basis or biological evidence to support race, and even less that defines one race as inferior to another.

GENDER

Grandma's Journey

My grandma had eight boys and two daughters who survived into adulthood. She lost around five children to miscarriage or early childhood death, and she herself passed away in my early childhood. I vividly remember her stories and the amazing hand weaving she did, turning old clothes into beautiful, embroidered blankets. Each of her grandkids received at least one such blanket as a gift from her. The one she gave me is a treasure, more precious to me now than I thought when I received it as a kid. (Like most kids, at the time I thought a toy car was much more interesting than a bedding item.)

When I think about it, my grandmother's whole life seemed to revolve around birthing and raising kids. My granddad passed away in his forties long before my birth. He worked in his farm part of the year, and spent the remaining months working on a cargo ship.

Much later in my childhood, my grandma moved around between her son's houses, changing her environment every six months or so. I used to look forward to our turn. I loved the homemade sweets she made and the blankets she embroidered, and I loved her stories about my dad, uncle, and aunts growing up as a family in the village they called home. Grandma never spoke about farming, travel, or politics. It had been decided for her long before that she would not understand or contribute to any of those areas. As a result, she only focused on kids, cooking, and sewing.

When my questions or curiosity went beyond scope of her usual stories, she would often say, "that's for the males of the house to figure out." So, in my young brain, all work which required physical strength and interaction outside the home became classified as "male jobs" by my grandma. No doubt this impression was reinforced by all the women in my family and community who stayed mostly at home. It was honestly not hard to convince a little boy that her way was the right way.

However, that is not her entire story.

I later learned that when political turmoil in the Indian subcontinent became unbearable, impacted as it was by the division of countries, food shortages, severe unemployment, and newly earned freedom, my ancestors grew desperate and struggled to survive. At that time my grandma (who I remember as physically small and frail, but extremely strong in character) was not expected to be capable of much that existed outside the home. That did not stop her from crossing an international border in middle of the night with her ten kids. She led them from their village in Bangladesh to a safer home in Calcutta, India.

I do not know whether she thought this fact was not worth mentioning or if she saw it as performing a "male role" in the face of an acute need. Perhaps she kept quiet because she did not want to take credit away from the males of the family. Either way, I am here in this world because of my grandma's bold and courageous move that night which she never took credit for.

Lessons in STEM

My mom is a very humble person and her educational background was not in the sciences. She was literature graduate and passed with minimum marks required. I, on the other hand, could do university level mathematics in high school, with ease.

Because my mom is humble, and did not have a STEM background, no one ever associates my mathematical acumen with her. She certainly never took any credit for it. Even my close family and friends did not realize she regularly taught me mathematics up to grade nine. Now, when I look back, I see how naturally hardworking and intelligent she is. She put energy into to learning something which she did not know well and committed herself to teaching me.

Knowing this about my mother helps me reflect on my wife and myself. My wife is much more talented and capable than me in many areas: public speaking, writing, leadership, and others. My wife is often addressed as Mrs. Bhaumik, though there is no 'Bhaumik' in her name. We did not think changing the last name was related to the success of our married life in any way.

Biology and Exclusion

For years, folks have claimed biology is the right reason to exclude women in various aspects of life. In today's language, gender has indeed been a partly social construct that follows women's traditional role: bearing children and serving as primary caregivers while men have been free to pursue positions of political, economic, and cultural power.

In fact, from the eighteenth century through modernity, legal constraints on Western women did not fall much short of de facto slavery. Mary Astell, often regarded as the first feminist (though she had precursors), made this point in response to John Locke's cramped endorsement of women's equality in his *Second Treatise*. "If all men are born free," she asks, "how is it that all women are born slaves?"[16]

In 1987, psychologist Alice Eagly *published Sex Differences in Social Behavior: A Social-Role Interpretation*, introducing a comprehensive theory of sex differences that embraces evolution, sociology, psychology, and biology.[17] In the beginning, it says, evolution led to

---

[16] *Some Reflections on Marriage*, 1700.

[17] Lawrence Erlbaum; 1st Edition. 1987.

physical sex differences. Males were larger, faster, and had greater upper body strength than females. Only females were capable of gestation and lactation. Given such differences, certain divisions of labor were natural in hunter-gatherer societies, and men's greater upper body strength funneled males into social roles involving physical strength and women into social roles involving childcare. Over the millennia, social roles gave rise to gender roles as people associated the behaviors of males and females with their dispositions. Social pressure followed. If society came to depend on women caring for children, little girls had to be socialized into the personality traits and skills that facilitate nurturance. If society has come to depend on men being providers and leaders, little boys needed to be socialized into the personality traits that facilitate acquiring resources and status.

From this incomplete understanding of biological differences, generation after generation justified the exclusion of women from the workplace. "Men and women selectively recruit hormones and other neurochemical processes for appropriate roles, in the context of their gender identities and others' expectations for role performance," Eagly and Wood write. In other words, biology interacts with psychology in two ways. Men and women psychologically internalize their gender roles as "self-standards" for regulating their behavior. They also regulate their behavior according to the expectations that others in the community have of them. Biology thus works with psychology to facilitate role performance.

Socialization theory refers to how children are exposed to influences that shape their gender identities. It recognizes that, until recent generations, little girls in the West were socialized, or taught how to be women, often by playing house and caring for their dolls. Pressure to comply with a gendered identity can come from parental interactions in infancy and toddlerhood, as girl babies are dressed differently from boy babies, and female toddlers are given dolls to play with while boys are given trucks. Or it may take the form of encouragement by parents, teachers, or playmates to engage in sex-typed play and eschew behaviors that go against that type, as in the case of tomboy girls and effeminate boys. Parents may teach different lessons about the right behavior, emphasizing the importance of being helpful and cooperative to daughters and the importance of standing up for themselves and taking the initiative for sons. Children may be encouraged to model themselves on the parent of their own sex.

In these and many other ways, sometimes subtle or unconscious, children constantly get signals that track with the stereotypes of males and females. This was true for my sister and my grandma. I am not placing blame—my parents and my sister did not realize what they were doing. They were just following what had been done till then.

Perhaps this also explains why my grandma not was big on talking about the fearless leadership she provided that night to save and provide a better life for her ten kids.

Today, our new reality is that the nature of most work and life has changed significantly. Machines and automation have taken over most heavy, hazardous work while humans are merely required to operate those machines or systems. Attributes like skill, knowledge, competency and accountability are much more important than upper body strength in most jobs. There is fundamentally no difference between the work I do compared to the work my wife and my sister do today.

Researchers have observed that the perceived differences between men and women in cognitive and verbal skills are overrated. In fact, a series of meta-studies analyzing hundreds of individual studies showed only a minimal difference between men and women—a conclusion that contradicts the notion that men are stronger thinkers and women are better verbally. Where differences have been found, the source of the difference is cultural.[18] This means these skills can be *developed*. An equitable policy will allow all to develop their skills and contribute to collaborative work.

---

[18] American Psychological Association, 2014.

This contradicts previous beliefs that women have stronger skills in reading non-verbal cues and that they are better at taking turns in conversation, which helps them make the most of the group's combined knowledge and skills. If a difference exists, it is slight. Consider the implications. If women are just as good as men in thinking and may even have a slight edge in empathy and inter-personal communication, why wouldn't they be welcome in work in all spheres ?

Finally, consider another fundamental change that has happened in human society: the prolific advancement of medical sciences. My grandma conceived fifteen times. My wife and I did once. We can go online and look up our vaccine record and do annual medical tests. Progress of medical sciences might seem unrelated on the surface, but they have profoundly affected our efforts at equity. We will not talk a lot more about medical sciences and their impact in our lives across world, but I encourage you to keep that in context as you read on.

CLASS

My First Driver's License

On a Sunday morning when I was seventeen I mentioned to my dad that I planned to get my driver's license. I still remember the long, heartfelt laugh my comment elicited.

My dad was never a discouraging parent. However, because we belonged to a certain stratum of society there was hardly any probability that I would ever own a vehicle of my own. The thought that we might own a vehicle one day was simply beyond the stretch of his imagination. He did not lack confidence in me; rather, his ideas about what was possible for our family were formed by a sense of 'class' that limits imagination and poten-tial. Years later, I had a dedicated car with a chauffeur for him. He never said anything to me about it. But my mom told me that every time they got in the car together, he said, "Our son is a good person. We raised him well." I wish he said that to me once. It means a lot to me. Maybe we broke the glass ceiling of class he thought would trap our family forever.

Legacies of Disadvantage

A person's social class origins leave a cultural imprint that has a lasting effect, even if the individual gains money or status later in life. In recent research, Jean Oh of Carnegie Mellon University found that U.S. workers from lower social-class origins are 32 percent less likely to become managers than people from higher origins. This disadvantage is even greater than that experienced by women compared with men (27 percent) or Blacks compared with whites (25 percent). And it prevails in every major economy in the world.[19]

The disadvantage matters—for individuals, organizations, and society. For individuals, class disadvantage materially limits career potential and the general well-being that comes from pay and promotion. To put this in perspective, consider the fact that researchers have found promotion to a managerial role creates substantial job satisfaction—as much as a 60 percent raise in pay would.

Class disadvantage matters for organizations because it excludes an entire group of people that may produce better-than-average leaders to fill the ranks of management. A study using data from the U.S. military, for example, suggests that individuals with lower social-class origins are less self-centered, which sets them up to be more effective as leaders. Similarly, a UK study found that lawyers from less-elite backgrounds are more motivated and capable than their privileged peers.

Class disadvantage matters for society because it means many workers do not have the opportunity to contribute to economic growth to their full potential. This is true of any disadvantaged group, but it's notably so in the case of social class, given that most people in the workforce have lower social-class origins. In representative

---

[19] Academy of Management, March 2022.

samples, more Americans identify as the "lower or working" class than the "middle or upper" class. Only a quarter of American adults today were raised by a parent with a degree, and by that measure, *three-quarters of adults* fall into the lower social-class origins category. Inability to create equitable environments for people who come from a lower social class, we are unable to engage majority of the eligible workforce. That is a grossly harmful indulgence, especially considering what happens if you do have equity..

Any hopes we might have of addressing racial inequity in the workplace require a clear-eyed analysis of its root causes—and these are increasingly connected to social class.[20] But in 2020, not one of the companies on Diversity Inc's "Top 50 Companies for Diversity" mentioned social class in their diversity, inclusion, and equity (DEI) goals and programs. Those companies paid a lot of attention to gender and race. Twitter, Facebook, Netflix, Google, and Amazon have all established employee resource groups (ERGs) to support employees from racial minorities or other underrepresented groups (Google alone has sixteen), but again, very few address social class.

As Harvard sociologist William Julius Wilson points out, racial disadvantages are intertwined with social class disadvantages, so remediations of the former are impossible without attention to the latter. One aspect of this phenomenon is centered around educational disadvantages. Workers with lower social-class origins tend to be less educated. Jean Oh explains that this accounts for about 60 percent of the disadvantages they experience in the workplace. But that disparity in education levels has often nothing to do with intelligence. As is the case for women and racial minorities, it has much more to do with context, expectations, and what's known as "stereotype threat"— the well-documented phenomenon whereby people perform worse because of the negative stereotypes attached to their identity. When people from lower social-class origins are inoculated against negative stereotypes, they perform just as well as others on intelligence tests.[21]

---

[20] Harvard Business Review, January–February 2021.

[21] PBS.org.

Is class a function of privilege, then? We know class is indeed a function of wealth. The system is biased in favor of the rich, who pass their money to the next generation, who in turn become the next generation of the upper class. A more nuanced viewpoint states social mobility has diminished in recent decades, which is symptomatic of an entrenched upper class.

Meanwhile, those who self-identify as conservatives commonly believe that class is a function of character, determination, and hard work. It draws from the traditional American credo: in America, people can become anything they want to be if they work hard enough. This is to say that people may differ in their talents, but for most occupations and roles in life innate talent is not nearly as important as character, determination, and hard work. One of my favorite books of all time on this topic is Geoff Colvin's *Talent is Overrated*. The book provides several examples and explanations to illustrate that it is usually deliberate practice which makes the difference, not so called "talent." As parents we often mentioned a kid to be talented on some skills and put a tag on it. My nine-year-old plays pretty good chess for his age. I often hear he is talented I think he is curious and interested and has put several hours on this game over last five years.

Two leading scholars of intersectionality theory, Margaret Andersen and Patricia Collins, say

> *Fundamentally, race, class, and gender are intersecting categories of experience that affect all aspects of human life; they simultaneously structure the experiences of all people in this society. At any moment, race, class, or gender may feel more salient or meaningful in a given person's life, but they are overlapping and cumulative in their effects. Together, the dimensions of intersectionality combine to form what Andersen and Collins labeled a matrix of domination.[22]*

---

[22] https://www.law.columbia.edu/news/archive/kimberle-crenshaw-intersectionality-more-two-decades-later

Class is driven by white privilege and the oppression of the patriarchy. Among psychologists who are familiar with the data, such views are exasperating but still underpin the foundations of their work. Psychologists' debates about heritability generally grow from common understandings. Francis Galton was the first person to try to study heritability scientifically. His book *Hereditary Genius* (1869) presented evidence from British history that people with excellence in the same field—judges, parliamentarians, poets, scientists, even wrestlers and oarsmen—tended to be related by blood. Twentieth-century scientists took up where they left off. The intuitive thought here is that if genes are important, people who are more closely related will resemble each other more—siblings will resemble each other more than half-siblings, for example.

A Way Forward

In the last half of the 20th century, technology, the economy, and the legal system became more complex, making it even more important for us to grasp and understand these complexities. Class has now become something to be addressed through equity drivers like education. Higher education itself has become accessible to everyone with enough cognitive ability. The most prestigious schools, formerly training grounds for children of the socioeconomic elite, began to be populated by students in the top few percentiles of IQ, no matter their family background.

Education—or more importantly, *knowledge*—ultimately becomes the glass ceiling-breaker for those held back by class. Knowledges makes it possible for a little boy who crossed the border with nine other siblings and his mom to become an accountant, own a house, and raise two decent kids alongside his strong wife. But possible does not mean easy, and that little boy, my dad, had a difficult time travelling from one level to the next. Ideas about where he fit into society held him back. Still, he crossed a great distance in a single lifetime. Now I pick up where he left off and continue the journey.

Business Sense Too

The earliest advocates for socialism supported meritocracy, where each person is rewarded for their ability and performance. That plank of equity served as the foundation of socialism but was ultimately replaced by equality and uniformity. Meanwhile, it has emerged as the central plank in the capitalists' playbook. The term *American Dream* was coined by James Truslow Adams in 1931 and accompanied with the saying that "life should be better and richer and fuller for everyone, with opportunity for each according to ability or achievement regardless of social class or circumstances of birth."[23]

The good news is that companies increasingly understand the value of equitable policies in recruiting and retaining diverse employees, as these workers play a critical role in a company's ability to adapt, grow and sustain a competitive advantage in the modern business landscape.

However, some companies fail to recognize the benefits of having a racially and ethnically diverse workforce. Factors such as prejudice and stereotypes towards certain racial or ethnic groups, whether conscious or subconscious, can lead to discriminatory practices in hiring.

To combat prejudice and internal resistance, companies need to appreciate the business case for diversity by outlining the benefits of a racially, ethnically, and gender-diverse workplace:

- Gains in worker welfare and efficiency,
- Reduced turnover costs,
- Fewer internal disputes and grievances,
- Improved accessibility to new and diverse customer markets,
- Higher productivity and increased revenue,
- Increased innovation,
- Development of new products and services,

---

[23] Lesson Plan: The American Dream". Library of Congress. Retrieved October 30, 2020.

- Improved company reputation management,
- Greater flexibility and adaptability in a globalized world,
- More efficient risk management (e.g. legal risks due to non-compliance),
- Prevention of marginalization and exclusion of categories of workers,
- Improved social cohesion, etc.

CONCLUSION

It is important to understand diversity from the lens of biology, psychology, and sociology. It is more important to appreciate that while all three help explain various aspects of diversity, they should not be an excuse for rejecting equity.

In other words, we can spend a lot of time in history to better understand what went wrong or right. Or we can focus on current contexts instead and do it right this time.

The work left for us now is to create equal opportunities with intent and apply equity as the glue that makes diversity beautiful and valuable.

KEY TAKEAWAYS

- Understanding the biology of human diversity is important, but often overlooked in discussions about diversity.
- Better understanding of the sources and history of diversity should help us better plan the journey of equity.
- Equity is that glue that makes diversity beautiful and useful.

CHAPTER 3:

DIVERSITY IS REALITY

Recently I showed drafts of the first two chapters of this manuscript to my wife. She said, "Diversity of ability is real. Make sure you spend time on that, too."

My wife is very passionate about accessible housing and facilities. She is on the board of a not-for-profit organization that focuses on accessible housing for people with diverse abilities due to age, accidents, or other reasons. Her passion comes, in part, from her friendship with an extremely talented and differently abled colleague who had an accident early in life. This person is lovely and a very successful professional, and her experience makes my wife's work even more real for her. While writing this chapter, I also thought about my aging mom and her needs. Health and abilities multiply the breadth of diversity in humans.

In this chapter I will try to provide a panorama of diversity, from the easy-to-see identifiers like gender and skin color to recognizing the full range of beliefs, values, and abilities. This overview includes some statistics and numbers as well. Hopefully this allows us to see that we live in a much more diverse world than most of us recognize.

In fact, as I explored the breadth of diversity it became very clear to me that no list is actually complete. Instead, our work is about keeping an open mind and appreciating diversity's breadth. To that end, I begin by painting few different dimensions of diversity with varying levels of detail to suggest its scope. I will address actionable ideas in later chapters.

Dimensions of Diversity

In attempt to give some structure to diversity's breadth, I am going to categorize its dimensions into four groups: *environmental*, *organizational*, *social*, and *individual*. All these dimensions impact us to different extents at different times and shape our behaviors and thinking.

- Environmental diversities include macro dimensions: political states, weather patterns, inflation, wars, pandemics, labor market, and etc.

- Organizational diversities refer to the entity-level dimensions within an organization: organizational culture, core values, organizational financial and reporting structures, department

Dimensions of Diversity

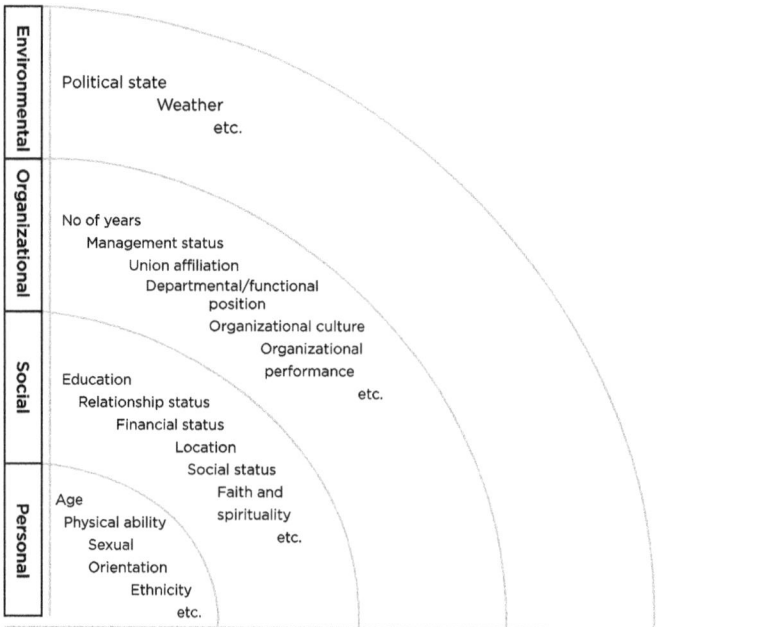

structures, and the like. (Interestingly if you replace organization with family or community, the same thinking applies.)

- Social dimensions include educational background, social status, religious faith, and etc.
- Finally, the personal dimension group addresses core attributes like age, physical ability, sexual orientation, and etc.

ENVIRONMENTAL DIVERSITY

Having worked in many large global organizations, I can attest to how fascinating it is to observe the influence outside factors have on its people and on the performance of the organization itself across multiple geographies. These factors often contribute to uniqueness within the same organization in different jurisdictions and countries. Since individuals working at organizations are part of the larger ecosystem, it is also very important to appreciate these dimensions for better context.

Weather Patterns

Let's start with some very simple examples like weather patterns. For folks like us who live in Canada, summer is our time go outdoors, take time off, and enjoy the natural landscape. This is when schools schedule their longest breaks and people are expected to be away, perhaps even working a bit slower. But in tropical climates, winter is the season folks look forward to for being outdoors. As a result, a lot more leave and family time occur over this part of the year. Clearly seasons corelate with the diverse moods, availability, and productivity of a workforce based on its geographic location. Like everything else in this chapter that context of diversity as an example is important to be aware of.

Pandemic Responses

The pandemic forced organizations to deal with new diversities triggered by novel medical and political situations. Even in the United States, very different perspectives on vaccination and lockdown emerged between states and political leadership, indicating vast ideological diversities inside a single country. There were also clear and unclear regulations across the world. Many large global organizations had to invest in large teams to ensure their compliance with authorities, society, and their employees. As the pandemic lingered, diverse political and medical viewpoints resulted in diverse perspectives on vaccination from employees within individual organizations. Viewpoints became so diversified that many organizations were forced to let people go and many employees passionately acted according to choices that risked their livelihood. I always wonder what verdict history will pass on all those organizational decisions several years from now.

Labor Market Diversity

Political intent often shapes the demographic composition of a population across regions. Residents of the United States are more racially and ethnically diverse today than ever, and this diversity continues to accelerate.

By 2055, the U.S. will not have a single racial or ethnic majority. Much of this change has been and will continue to be driven by immigration, and immigration policies have been driven by the changing political scenario. With more and more American-born Asians and Indians today holding important positions in the U.S. government, a near-record 14 percent of the country's population is foreign-born compared with just 5 percent in 1965. Over the next five decades, the majority of U.S. population growth is projected to be linked to new Asian and Hispanic immigration.

Historically, white Americans have made up a majority of the U.S. population. In 1965, they registered over 80 percent. Today, that number has shrunk to approximately 60 percent and is projected to decrease to only 46 percent by 2065. That still leaves white Americans as the largest population, but by a much smaller margin than a century earlier. Meanwhile, the Black population remains approximately the same while the Hispanic and Asian populations are projected to triple. Asian populations are also projected to surpass Hispanic populations.

Immigration

Immigration plays a critical role in these shifting percentages. The Hispanic population is expected to decrease from approximately 45 percent of total immigrants to only 31 percent by 2065. Meanwhile, Asians increase by approximately 10 percent. Also, the number of white immigrants has already dropped significantly from 1965 to 1995. Once accounting for 80 percent of all immigrants, by 1995 they accounted for only 25 percent.

Voting and Legislation

While population gains and losses are significant, the power to pass legislation rests in the voting activity of each population. Historically, white populations have voted in higher numbers in the U.S. than Black, Asian, and Hispanic populations. Consider that only about 50 percent of registered voters turn out for a presidential election and even fewer for midterm, state, and local elections.

As the political environment of a country changes, so do the diversity statistics in the workforce. Politics influence corporate policies in every country. That's why all large corporations have a government relationship department. Based on the nature of the industry and its regulatory aspects, this could be more important for some organizations than others.

Corporate Equity Legislation

Legislation is one of the most common tools governments use to drive corporate behaviors. A review of a few legislations illustrates how the government has established rules by which companies must operate within the United States.

California has adopted two board diversity statutes. The first, SB 826, requires publicly held companies (defined as corporations listed on major U.S. stock exchanges) with principal executive offices in California, no matter where they are incorporated, to include minimum numbers of women on their boards of directors. Under the law, each of these publicly held companies was required to have a minimum of one woman on its board of directors by the close of 2019. That minimum increased to two by December 31, 2021, if the corporation has five directors, and three women directors if the corporation has six or more total directors.

- Washington State enacted the Washington Business Corporation Act (WBCA) in June 2020 that mandates public companies have a "gender-diverse board" of 25 percent women by January 1, 2022.

- Colorado and Pennsylvania passed legislation encouraging companies to support an increase in the number of women on boards.

- Several other states—Hawaii, Massachusetts, Michigan, Ohio, and New Jersey—have introduced legislation addressing minimum board diversity requirements but have yet to pass formal actions.

- In Canada, TSX Boards made small but steady strides towards increasing women representation on boards in 2019. Of about 600 TSX companies reporting women board director data, the percentage of all-male boards decreased to 15.7 in mid-year 2021, down from 18.3 percent in mid-2020 and 20 percent at the beginning of 2020. Women held only 21.2 of all board seats. The Utilities and Pipelines industry continues to have the highest average percentage of women on their boards (35 percent). The average number of women on boards of all companies disclosing data increased modestly from 1.69 in 2020 to 1.83 in 2021.

- In Europe, women held 29.5 percent of board seats in the largest publicly listed companies in EU member states in 2020. In the largest listed companies in the six Member States with mandated quotas, women comprised 37.6 percent of board seats.

In countries without these hard mandates, only 24.3 percent of board members were women. Less than 1 in 10 women were board chairs or CEOs.

Corporate Boards and Diversity

Are these regulations, combined as they are with some amount of intent from organizations, really working? Let's look at some stats.

Legislation, social pressure, and a genuine desire for inclusivity are changing Fortune 500 and Fortune 100 corporate boards. According to a Corporate Governance survey by Cydney Posner on June 9, 2021, there is a trend for including gender, race, and color.

In March 2021, Nasdaq required at least two diverse directors on their boards. If they did not meet that objective, they would need to explain their rationale for not doing so.

- Two hundred Fortune 500 companies reflect more than 40 percent diversity on their boards, almost four times the number of companies a decade ago.

- In June 2021, women and racial/ethnic minorities represented 42.2 percent of directors the on boards of Fortune 100 companies, and about 38 percent of directors on boards of Fortune 500 companies. In addition, slightly more than 20 percent of board seats in the Fortune 100 were held by racial/ethnic minorities, while the percentage was only 18 percent among the Fortune 500. The rate of increase for racial/ethnic minorities in the 2018-2020 period was slightly below 0.5 percent, a rate that would not achieve a level of 40 percent representation of minorities until 2055.

- This progress in overall diversity has been due primarily to an increase in the number of white women on boards, the group that experienced the biggest increase: a gain of 34 seats (15 percent) in the Fortune 100 and 209 seats (21 percent) in the Fortune 500. The conclusion is largely consistent with the conclusion from another study regarding board diversity in

California, where 90 percent of the gains for women on Fortune 100 boards between 2018 and 2020 were gains by white women.

- Among the Fortune 500, according to Posner's report, "for every board seat newly occupied by a minority woman, white women occupied nearly three new seats." Despite gender diversity's upward trend, ethnic and racial diversity still need attention.

- Since 2004, gains for women and racial/ethnic minorities have averaged under 2 percent per year, with representation on boards of the Fortune 100 essentially unchanged for minority men and only slightly improved (0.5 percent) for minority women. At that rate, Posner's report estimates, the representation of minority women on Fortune 100 boards will be about 20 percent of the U.S. adult population until 2046.

- For Black directors, just over two out of every five board seats (43 percent) were held by a single director serving on multiple Fortune 500 boards. That percentage was only 23 percent for directors who are Asian and Pacific Islanders.

- Of the 974 board seats filled by new directors among the Fortune 500 since 2018, 81 percent were filled by white directors, 53.8 percent of which were filled by white men. Concerning new directors on Fortune 100 boards, 79.9 percent were filled by white directors, including 52.1 percent filled by white men (a slight increase from 2018).

- The Report identified 29 companies in the Fortune 500 that demonstrated at least 60 percent board diversity (the highest percentage of women and racial/ethnic minority representation). However, the Report found no companies that reflected the demographics of the U.S., with the benchmarks of 50 percent women, 13 percent Black, 18 percent Hispanic, and 6 percent Asian/Pacific Islander.

As you can see, some of the data above is a year or so old. Regardless, the statistics depict a trend of increasing diversity for women and minority groups in executive boards. That is good news because it shows progress. However, the work is not completed. There isn't statistical equality yet.

Summary

Environmental drivers often appear to be macro level and extraneous to the organization. But contextual awareness is relevant and important for understanding the diversity landscape in which an organization operates. Impact of environmental dimension will only increase over time for organizations particularly the larger ones.

ORGANIZATIONAL DIVERSITY

I began my career as a Tech entrepreneur. After exiting from that venture, I spent a couple of decades working for large consulting organizations like IBM, Siemens, and CGI. During that period I performed different roles in different industries. I was always surprised at the way organizations were so unique in terms of their DNA and culture.

Some organizations cared more and were more conscious of their employees' seniority than others. Some did not care much about tenure and were hyper focused on metrics that drove revenue and profitability. In some organizations, sales departments were the epicenter and exerted the most influence over the company. On the other hand, a large energy midstream company was dominated by its finance department. Most organizations talked about employee wellness. Some really meant what they said. Others cared about numbers and targets far more than anything else.

Once I was having some serious issues with a large transformation project. Most of the difficulty was centered around a third-party partner's inability to dedicate resources so they could meet their responsibilities and scope around a payment system. I spoke with senior executives in charge of delivery, but had limited success. Going up the chain on the delivery side of their organization was not enough. The impact and stakes were high: the significant burn rate for the project experienced several delays, and on top of that, we lacked the working payment solutions necessary to have in place before our Black Friday sale. Both would eventually impact the business if not addressed before the sale. I was trying to find a solution to the problem, but I did not know what else to do. I was already regularly to talking to their global EVP of delivery.

I started reaching out, informally, through my personal contacts. I spoke to a few peer organizations who had recently implemented the same solution from the same supplier. I soon learned that others had faced similar issues during their own implementations. One of the gentlemen I talked with suggested that I contact the EVP of Sales. The advice seemed unusual to me at the time, but I followed it. Once my problem became a concern for the EVP of Sales, everything changed. We connected well, he was incredibly helpful, and the issues I'd been facing turned around.

It became obvious to me then that sales departments drive this organization's business in a much bigger way than I'd ever realized. I also learned that individuals within that company who held similar titles had significantly different influences: not every Executive Vice President held the same sway. After further digging I came to know that the EVP of Delivery had indeed been trying to help, but his words simply did not have the same effect as those of the EVP of Sales.

In other words, within every organization there are two critical structures at play—an organizational structure and a structure of influence—and they do not always correspond in the way you might expect.

Take a moment to reflect that thought in your world. I am confident you will find some examples of this very thing. You might even notice, as I did, that the pattern changes with organizations and countries.

These diversities in each organization's way of life have always fascinated me. It is interesting to observe the shifts as different groups dominate influence and others recede into the background of operations. When the sales department drives decision-making, for example, other departments like finance and engineering find themselves being told what to do.

That said, it is important to remember that employees from all departments have their own personal, diverse sense of ownership, authority, and accountability. This kind of diversity is over and above usual considerations of gender, race, and class, because it exists at an intersection between where one belongs in an organization and the power spectrum within that organization. It could be as simple as titles and the authorities that come with them, as perceived by stakeholders and others in the organization. Importantly, equity enablement should give voice across hierarchy and across departments. This is where culture plays a bigger role.

Sources of Organizational Diversity

At an individual level, diversity in an organization often emerges through the following parameters:

- Seniority and length of tenure with the company
- Management status
- Union affiliation
- Department/functional position
- Organization culture
- Organizational performance

Another interesting source and contributor for organizational diversity is Merger and Acquisition (M&A). In this sense, diversity and inclusion stretch beyond the traditional boundaries of DEI. "Our people" and "their people" are consumed by conversations that will ultimately include some and exclude others.

Discouragingly, research shows a very large percentage of failure rate for mergers and acquisitions: upward of 50 percent overall. That is a remarkably high figure, but considering the range of business, technology, and cultural factors that occur during the average merger or acquisition, it is not that surprising. Part of the problem is creating a new company from two different cultures. Establishing a productive and profitable company by creating a diverse team with distinctly different cultures can be very difficult.

As they say, "Culture eats strategy for breakfast." Similarly, organizational DNA, culture, and way of working creates a unique diversity within an organization which is often not visible through universal lenses like gender, color of skin, or disability. As an organization matures in their understanding of diversity in general, it is very important that it understands its own diversities, which are created from within.

SOCIAL DIVERSITY

Social diversity is that which we all inherit from the society we belong to or operate in. As we discussed in Chapter 2, class is a major driver of social diversity. Educational background, financial means, relationships, and faith contribute to social diversity as well. In this section we will explore these aspects to make us conscious and aware of the diversities presented by society at large.

Education

Even in a developed country like the U.S., where access to primary education is free, one finds diversity in education, degrees, and higher education.

A report from US Census Bureau highlights the diversity in education from different parts of the U.S. population:

- Over the past 15 years, the number of Americans holding at least a bachelor's degree has steadily increased, a trend that holds up for every racial and ethnic group.[24]

---

[24] Bachelor's Degree Attainment in the United States: 2005 to 2019 in U.S. Census Bureau. https://www.census.gov/library/publications/2021/acs/acsbr-009.html

- The percentage of the population 25 years and older that holds at least a bachelor's degree has increased by about 5 percentage points over the last 15 years.

- Between 2005 and 2009, 27.5 percent of this group had a bachelor's degree. That increased to 29.3 percent between 2010 and 2014. From 2015 to 2019, the percentage reached 32.1 percent.

- The percentage of adults with a bachelor's degree increased for all racial/ethnic groups, but attainment gaps by race persist.

- The bachelor's degree attainment by racial group between 2015 to 2019:
  - Asian: 54.3 percent
  - White: 33.5 percent
  - Black: 21.6 percent
  - Native Hawaiian/Other Pacific Islander: 17.8 percent
  - Hispanic/Latino: 16.4 percent
  - American Indian/Alaska Native: 15.0 percent
  - Other: 12.0 percent
  - Two or more races: 31.9 percent

While Blacks and Pacific Islanders lead the increase, the number of people in those groups with a bachelor's degree is still in the minority.

Within an organization, informal groups often form between those with similar educational backgrounds. There is nothing wrong with that; it is normal for community to form around commonalities. However, it is also important to appreciate education-based diversities that exist in the workplace and recognize that equity for these groups is not optional.

For example, consider the implementation of new technology projects. If you have experienced difficult circumstances as a result of new tech in your organization, you might not be an exception. Most big organizations experience difficulty when they implement new technology solutions. New technology often comes with new process and creates a learning curve for frontline workers that can seem frustrating at best or impossible at worst. Some of this challenge is inevitably part of a major change, while other challenges can be addressed by designing solutions with users as the center: from the outside in. Thankfully, human-first design is mitigating these effects in the organizations that utilize it. It is about appreciating the diversity of thinking between users and builders and designing with users at the epicenter.

Relationship Status

When you think of a family, what do you envision? Is your picture of the typical nuclear family a mom, dad, and two kids? Or do you picture an entirely different family structure—one that more closely resembles the families you've come to know and perhaps even grown up in yourself?

As with marital status, our understanding of "family" is evolving; the traditional family structure known as the nuclear family in the U.S. has already changed. The following data highlights the diversity in relationship status:

- According to PEW Research Center, in 1990 67 percent of the U.S. population was married and 29 percent was unpartnered. In 2019, 53 percent were married and 38 percent unpartnered. That is a reduction of 14 percent in the married population and an increase of 9 percent in the unpartnered population.[25]

- Same sex marriage has increased approximately 70 percent in the U.S. since the Supreme Court decision in 2015. By 2020, 58 percent of LBGQ couples were married.[26]

- Interracial marriages grew from 3 percent of marriages in 1967 to 20 percent in 2020 in the United States. Meanwhile, today, 94 percent of the population approves. This is due to an increasingly diverse population and increased education.[27]

---

[25] PEW **Research.org**, October 6, 2021.

[26] leearningenglish.ovanews.com

[27] Axios.com

These changes are already being reflected in marketing and other profit-driving organizational strategies. For example, say you are launching a new product like a car or vacation package. Before, targeting advertising to a family with mom, dad, two kids and a dog was universal and largely unquestioned. In North America, the same could be said about marketing to a family with white skin color. Now, however, because of our understandings of the dimensions of diversity, and including them in market research to a target customer, those demographics are no longer uniform. These days it is common for an advertisement to feature families that include mixed-race and/or same-sex couples, sometimes with their children and sometimes without.

The same logic should guide the way we conduct daily organizational operations as we focus on meeting the needs of a relationally diverse workforce.

Financial Status

In its purest form, income is the money we receive for our work. However, income is also much more than that. It often determines the neighborhood we live in, the types of schools we have access to, and our healthcare options. Our income shapes our interactions with the criminal justice system and determines what retired life will look like. It is more than just the money we receive for our work. That means financial status is an extremely diverse concept.

A series of reports by Pew Research Centre shows the changing of income in the U.S.:

- The U.S. middle class decreased from 60 percent in 1971 to 50 percent in 2021.[28]
- The U.S. upper class increased from 14 percent in 1971 to 21 percent in 2021.

---

[28] Pew **Research.org**, 2022.

- The U.S. lower class increased from 25 percent in 1971 to 29 percent in 2021.
- While incomes have risen for the middle class, they have not kept pace with rising incomes of the upper class.

Financial diversity within an organization can be significant. Employees working in the same organization often would have significant spread in their earnings, bonuses, and financial means, leading to lifestyles with high diversity.

Faith and Spirituality

Few topics will cause alienation quicker than politics and religion. In our quest to "do it right" with diversity and inclusion, matters of faith and spirituality are not insignificant.

A religious belief is defined as the attitude towards a religion's central articles of faith. One example of this is the Christian belief that Jesus is the son of God. While all religions have prescribed beliefs, not all individuals who identify with that religion adopt these beliefs. In 2020, 83 percent of the world's population identified as following one of 12 major religions, which shows a plethora of diversity: Baha'i, Buddhism, Christianity, Confucianism, Hinduism, Islam, Jainism, Judaism, Shinto, Sikhism, Taoism, Zoroastrianism. Depending on the interpretation of a religious belief, agnosticism/atheism (the absence of belief in a higher power) may be the thirteenth major religion.

Notice the significance of that number. More than 8 out of 10 people claim to follow a religion.

Then notice that *which* religions individuals choose to follow are changing, to the point that the world's religious makeup will look very different by 2050. Over the next two-and-a-half decades, Christianity will remain the largest religious group, but Islam will grow faster than any other major religion. By 2050, the number of people declaring themselves as Muslims will nearly equal that of Christians. In the U.S., the Muslim population will remain small but is projected to grow rapidly.

When it comes to dealing with matters of diversity at work, faith is one aspect that is neglected.

Summary

Organization operates within a society or even in multiple social constructs based on how large and spread it is. Social diversities that exists in the organization are a subset of the society in which it operates. Whether it comes to local policies, branding, or product mix, the social dimension of diversity plays a big role.

PERSONAL DIVERSITY

Every employee brings a unique combination of diverse elements to the workplace. Understanding the equity each provides is the secret to a quality hire and productive employee. In the following section, we discuss several of these elements (beyond gender and race), ranging from age to ability, and explore a few other attributes of personal diversity which might not always be as broadly discussed.

Age

People of different ages give different values to the company, each providing a very important marker for a company's development in the future.

At a very basic level, younger employees bring energy to the workplace, along with fresh ideas and technological savvy. But they often need the wisdom and accumulated knowledge of the more seasoned worker. Older employees provide a combination of acquired knowledge and industry experience, a balance of perspective, and common sense that becomes wisdom. By working together, the organization gains the best of both worlds. However, when allowed to separate into polarized generations, tension tears apart potential gains. A Randstad study found that generations working together yielded an 83 percent increase in innovation. Therefore, a range of ages in combination with each other creates a vibrant and valuable benefit for the organization.[29]

Research shows that age-diversified work teams—those comprised of multi-generational members—provide three critical elements:

- Promote sharing of best practices and different perspectives,
- Build a healthy pipeline for creating a healthy future-ready workforce, and
- Foster innovation.[30]

I can personally attest to the value in age-diversified work teams. In a later chapter, I talk about how a senior member of my team changed my leadership for better once I got over my discomfort with the age dimension of diversity.

The Deloitte Review Issue of 2021 shows that our current workplaces offer significant age diversity and, therefore, a wealth of potential innovation.

Labor force participation (actual and projected), by age group

Cohort	1994	2004	2014	2024
16 to 24	66.4%	61.1%	55.0%	49.7%
25 to 54	83.4%	82.8%	80.9%	81.2%
55 to 64	56.8%	62.3%	64.1%	66.3%
65 to 74	17.2%	21.9%	26.2%	29.9%
75 and older	5.4%	6.1%	8.0%	10.6%
Total	66.6%	66.0%	62.9%	60.9%

Source Bureau of Labor Statistics

Even with these shifts, the 25–54-year-old group will still make up the majority of the workforce, although the proportion of workers in this category will decline, as will the proportion of 16–24-year-olds

---

[29] Randstad.com

[30] Mycareersfuture.gov

(according to Bureau of Labor Statistics projections). The only age group projected to gain a share between 2014 and 2024 is the 55-and-over age group.

If you are a leader in a corporation, this signals a beneficial trend. Older workers hold considerable intellectual capital that benefits your organization. Learn to leverage that knowledge. Also, leverage their ability to balance the enthusiastic and technical knowledge of the younger workers.

Meanwhile, note that the number of workers 25-54 will decrease. That is partly because there are now so many more ways to become an entrepreneur. The internet allows each of us to start a business, grow an audience, and make a living wage in our spare time. That is different than before the year 2000, when it was much more difficult.

Changing Trends

Current trends in business and technology show that the way employees work — where, when, why, and with whom — will change completely over the next decade and bear little resemblance to work as it stands today.[31]

Over the next several years the way of working will significantly change the role of middle management. Currently, teams comprise a group of people pulled together by reporting structure or ad hoc fashion. Teamwork is therefore considered more of a behavioral necessity than a legitimate organizational principle. In the past, teamwork has been designed primarily to foster team spirit and collaboration. However, by 2030, the complexity and scale of business objectives will demand the involvement of brain power and expertise across boundaries in more intricate ways. Employees will use avatars, language software, conversational interfaces, and real-time dialect translation to work and speak

---

[31] Top Ten Technologies Driving the Digital Workplace. https://www.gartner.com/smarterwithgartner/top-10-technologies-driving-the-digital-workplace

with team members. That will require a different approach to business, especially in large corporations.

Looking ahead, we see that the number of workers will increase by five billion between 2017 and 2037. But notice much of this 14 percent increase in workers comes from Africa. Think and appreciate the DEI aspects of that trend in our society and workforce.

Physical Ability

Earlier, we discussed how establishing equity is based on an individual's ability to provide value to the organization and society. Thus the issue of ability becomes a focal point in the discussion about inclusion, especially for those with a physical or mental disability.

Physical disability is a condition that negatively affects a person's stamina, dexterity, mobility, and/or physical capacity. These conditions range from hearing impairments to cerebral palsy. A mental disability is when a person cannot develop cognitively at the same rate as most others.

The Davos Economic Report of 2019 provides several critical points when contemplating the value of including individuals with different abilities in the workforce. Most importantly, they point to the facts: more than one billion people in this world are living with some form of disability (one in seven people). Eighty percent of these people acquire their disability between the ages of 18 and 64—the average working age for most—and they are 50 percent more likely to be unemployed.

In the US alone, there are 15.1 million working-age people living with visible and non-visible disabilities, many of whom are un- or underemployed. If companies embraced disability inclusion, they would gain access to a new talent pool of more than 10.7 million people.

The benefits of disability-inclusive hiring practices extend far beyond the bottom line. Studies show that working alongside employees with disabilities makes others more aware of how to make the workplace more inclusive and better for everyone. Staff turnover is also lower by up to 30 percent when a well-run disability community outreach program is in place.[32]

Thankfully, hiring workers with a disability has increased significantly. Today, many companies hire people with mental and physical disabilities and treat them equitably. Accessing a new pool of individuals who want to be involved has far-reaching potential to help expand the capabilities of any branch. Note that when we change our perspective to see how those we have previously dismissed can do far more than we expected, we discover valuable resources.

A survey by National Business and Disability Council in 2017 found that 66 percent of consumers will purchase goods and services from a business that features persons with disabilities in their advertising, while 78 percent will purchase goods and services from a business that takes steps to ensure easy access for individuals with disabilities at their physical locations.

Several companies are raising the bar for disability employment and inclusion. T-Mobile has started sponsoring National Wheelchair Basketball Association youth events, where staff speak with children about what it means to work at T-Mobile, opening children's eyes to new opportunities. Bank of America has created a support services team of 300 people with intellectual disabilities to manage fulfillment services and external client engagement.

In the United States, the Disabilities Act not only prohibits discrimination against qualified workers (a qualified worker is one who has the qualifications and abilities to perform the essential functions of the job) based on disability but also requires that employers make reasonable accommodation—that is, the employer provides a piece of equipment, changes non-essential job functions or makes some other adjustment that does not cause the employer undue hardship,

---

[32] Weforum.org

so the disabled employee can perform the essential functions of the job. This approach protects workers' rights and makes it "safe" to request accommodations.

Sexual Orientation

For the longest time blue was for boys and pink was for girls. When keen new parents wanted to decorate their baby's room before birth and/or sex determination, they would often flex to a green.

The world still finds it hard to accept the spectrum of color beyond this. It is a big change. It is hard for folks who are deciding and declaring themselves in the spectrum. We can also be hard on ourselves in two ways – one by resisting the obvious and on the other hand by judging people who are finding it hard to go through this new construct of society. It is hard for both.

The reality is humans have the right to choose their own sexual preferences. Like everything else in life, that might not align with our own orientation and comfort.

We have two choices. One, resist that acceptance and reduce our circle of diversity and create a world and workplace around us which does not represent society and reality. Two, accept and respect this as any other diversity dimension and help include it into our world and work.

While I believe the only choice is what I have outlined as the second one above, it is important to also understand that it might hard on many to accept this. We just talked about education as one of the attributes of diversity; we talked about age and others. Based on where one is in those other dimensions, one's ability to accept spectrum of sexual orientation might vary.

CONCLUSION

Diversity is broad. It can be a personal experience; it can even be a corporate requirement. Diversity includes those young and old, those with different physical abilities and sexual orientations, and the list goes on.

Diversity is a fact of life in the world, corporate workplaces, and personal life. Our world is diverse and also becoming more so.

KEY TAKEAWAYS

- Actual Dimensions of diversity are almost always broader than what an organization can focus on in its diversity performance indicators.
- Whatever your lens of diversity, in almost all cases the ecosystem will get more diverse in the future.
- A list of the dimensions of diversity can be very big and never complete. It is all about acknowledging the breadth of difference with openness and a willingness to accept new dimensions when we encounter them.

CHAPTER 4:

I USED TO BE MAJORITY

Our journey continues with a necessary but unexpected detour into the ways in which some efforts of inclusion have threatened the inclusion of the current majority. To do it right, we must strike the delicate balance of including everyone, not just current minorities. Sometimes we rush to remedy, overcompensating to bring about short-term solutions while ignoring the long-term inequities.

I was a bit hesitant to even include this chapter. I second-guessed myself on the chapter title and the content. I worried that I would be misinterpreted as someone who does not advocate for inclusion of minority groups.

Eventually, I got past my hesitation. I am a visible minority where I live and work. I do understand and appreciate the value of equity initiatives for minority groups more than most. However, I felt obliged to put together a majority perspective and consideration based on two things: my own past experiences, and conversations with close friends who belong to visible majority groups.

All major corporations these days have multiple Employee Resource Groups (ERG) focused on minority groups (e.g., ERG for Persons of

Color; ERG for LGBTQ+, ERG for Women in Business, etc.). The ERG group concept is good as long as groups are structured well and promote safe conversation. But while ERG groups are supposed to make the target group more included and welcomed within an organization, how many of these organizations have an ERG group for white men? Not many. I have not experienced one. Does that mean most organizations in North America are unintentionally excluding their own majorities?

Often, it is assumed that since one is part of the *majority* group, he or she must feel comfortable, included, and engaged. I think this assumption is the biggest gap in the diversity and inclusion programs of most organizations. In the midst of so much change, white men are equally uncomfortable and need a safe space.

I applaud all organizations who have taken DEI initiatives focused on minority communities more seriously than ever before. I believe it is great and slowly but surely making an impact.

Having said that, this chapter is intended to bring the often-overlooked *inclusion* (or, more accurately, the *avoidance of exclusion*) of majority populations to the top of our minds.

Majority Thinking

I needed to explore the mind of the majority, who still often act from a place of bias and exclusion, to form a full picture of the problems surrounding diversity and inclusion. Although it would be easy to accept the bandwagon, politically correct explanation, I knew there were underlying issues that compelled individuals to not only passively resist inclusion, but to violently exclude minority members. I also knew that without understanding these issues, we would never get it right and change the course.

Once again, I draw from personal experience. Growing up in India, I was in the majority. When I moved to Canada, I immediately became the visible minority. I will try to traverse these perspectives side by side from that unique perspective, because I believe it is absolutely necessary to balance the same.

In high school, I had a lot of interests: a variety of sports, writing, reading, and motorbiking. My parents, of course, wanted me to focus primarily on education and prepare for the world. They knew one thing for sure: the probability breaking through the poverty ceiling would be embedded somewhere in the journey through higher education. After my high school, like most students with high professional aspirations, I decided to write competitive exams.

Most believe the path to quicker success will be found in STEM studies: physics, mathematics, engineering, or medicine. For that reason, I decided to write a competitive exam for medicine. The number of applicants was high, while only a low percentage of applicants would be accepted.

After waiting for about two months, the day of results finally came. It was a very rainy day. A printed list of successful candidates was published and hung up on the notice boards of the major medical colleges throughout the city. My friends and I journeyed through the rain and reached one such college, where a crowd had gathered around the list. My friend, who was keener than me, made his way to the front, dodging through the knot of umbrellas held aloft by parents and other hopeful candidates. My friend yelled to let me know that my name was indeed on the list of selected candidates, which meant my ranking was within the threshold of total seats available for admission.

For few minutes, it felt good to know I had made it. However, it dawned on me shortly afterward there was a "quota" factor. Some of the candidates with much lower ranks on the list would get better school choices than me because of these quotas.

Quota is a form of reservation wherein a percentage of seats in all government and competitive examinations is designated for people with certain backgrounds—those assumed to be "backward" and underprivileged. In India, those reservations were often based on caste and provided as equity measures that created opportunity for individuals from lower castes to participate in higher education.

The idea itself is great. It works in many ways. But because I belonged to the majority and general caste, I was not included in these reservations. My admission could be only based on merit. Again—in principle, there's nothing wrong with that. But I felt differently about it that day. The program meant to extend equity actually worked against me.

Interestingly, the list of candidates who got quota preference included a couple of students from my high school. From a purely merit-based perspective, their scores placed them farther down the list than me, but they got better college offers than I did because of the reservation system.

That's when I realized the real impact of quotas.

As of July 2022, India's president is a female of minority origin. I am very proud of this fact. It is historical in many ways that the world's largest democracy got its first female president from a backward caste. Droupadi Murmu was sworn in on July 25, 2022.

Besides being only the second female president of India, Ms. Murmu, who until recently was the governor of Jharkhand State, will be the first from the country's Indigenous tribal communities, an economically marginalized population that makes up nearly 10 percent of India's population.

There is no question that reservations helped folks who otherwise would have had a much longer journey to equity. But at that moment, on that rainy day, I felt wronged.

To be candid, I found it very hard to accept when the system seemed to work against me. A classmate of mine who was at a lower rank was getting better choices because his last name indicated he was from a backward community, but I knew he had grown up with far more resources than I had. His dad probably made four times the income my dad made, for example.

It was not the intent of the quota system that galled me. It was how the system was implemented which made me feel absolutely excluded. It did not help that over the years I had watched helplessly as politicians added category after category to win votes—never mind that they reduced merit portions more and more.

When I reflect on the experience, I recognize the big picture. I judged folks on that day by taking their last names as evidence that their spot was not earned. I know better now. That was not fair, but it did cause the flip side of 'quotas' to dawn on me. It forced me to ask whether the majority population was being excluded.

Worse, that was the first time I started examining the surnames of each of my friends to find out if they belonged to a backward caste, and it is when the concept of categorization based on quotas became so evident. The experience created something almost like master data in my head; I did not do that consciously.

At the risk of being judged for admitting this, for a period of time I was stuck in a state of denial and the feeling that I had been wronged. I could not elevate myself easily from personal perspective to the larger cause. I could not name many examples in which the constraints I experienced while growing up were deeper and more hurtful than many getting the preference outside of merit list. It took some time for me to get over it.

So, what did the quotas do? I believe they created equity for people with lower abilities and resources, who did not have access to good education and resources, and gave them equal opportunity to participate in various things, which I think is very noble and the right thing to do.

However, I still feel the need to acknowledge that it also produced a different effect in my mind. I realized that if I decided to pursue an administrative services job in India, I would always have to fight the quota system. But quotas did not apply to the practices of the corporate world—the world I saw as a world of talent, and in which I still believe is a fantastic place to be. I decided to join the ranks of individuals who came to business to excel, and I don't regret my decision.

The Reservation Quota in India - by Category

Reservation Quotas in India - Present Scenario

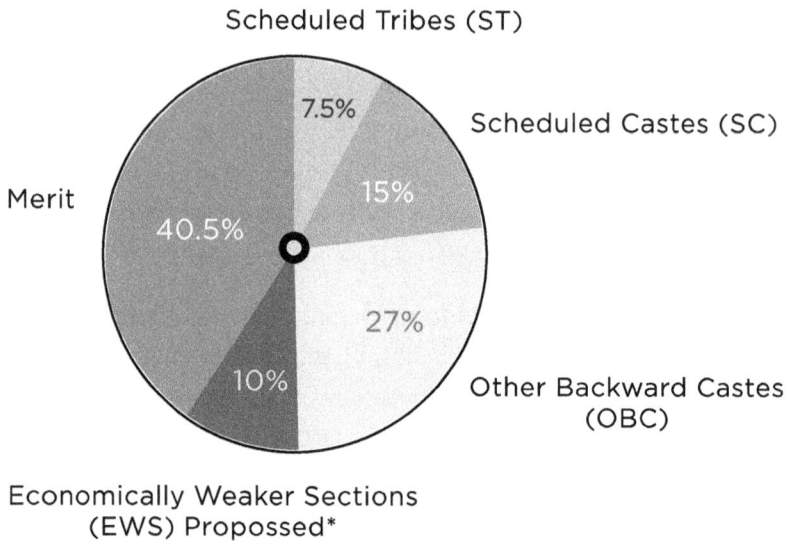

Scheduled Tribes (ST)

Scheduled Castes (SC)

7.5%

15%

Merit

40.5%

27%

10%

Other Backward Castes (OBC)

Economically Weaker Sections (EWS) Propossed*

A new Act based on the 124th Amendment Bill of 2019 was passed in the Indian Parliament that provides a 10 percent reservation to economically weaker sections (EWS) in the General category. The reservation of EWS of the general category is beyond existing quotas for SC (Scheduled Caste), ST (Scheduled Tribe), and OBC (Other Backward Class) people.

The Reservation Quota in India - Summary

Reservation In India - Merit vs. Reserved

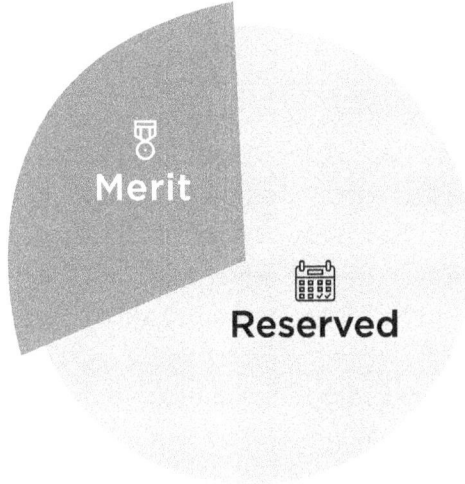

Merit

Reserved

At present, Reservations in India account for a total of 49.5 percent. If the 10 percent extra reservation for EWS is also considered, it would be 59.5 percent. The remaining 7.5 percent, 15 percent, and 27 percent quotas are reserved for Scheduled Tribes, Scheduled Castes, and Other Backward Classes, respectively.

Wider Applications

I made the decision to pursue Physics later. In hindsight, I do not believe I would be a good doctor.

If some of my readers from more advanced countries are tuning out now, thinking my experience in India is not relevant to theirs, they might be correct. But I have talked to many professionals in North America and know many are feeling the same way I did on that rainy day. The question is, are we leaving some feeling excluded from the majority group as we move? Are we focusing on everyone, or just immediately visible minorities as we look for quick wins?

Initiatives, Regulations, and Quotas for Minorities by the U.S. Government

In the United States, the journey to racial equity started with the Civil Rights Legislation in 1963. The Civil Rights Act of 1964 (pushed heavily and then signed by President Lyndon B. Johnson after John F. Kennedy's assassination) was the resulting law. Not only did it outlaw government discrimination and unequal application of voting qualifications by race, it—for the first time—also outlawed segregation and other forms of discrimination by most businesses that were open to the public, including hotels, theaters, and restaurants. It also outlawed discrimination on basis of race, ethnicity, religion, sex, or national origin by most employers.

Today, the Equal Employment Opportunity Commission (EEOC) monitors employment discrimination claims and helps enforce this provision of the law in favor of minorities.

The Urban League and the National Association for the Advancement of Colored People (NAACP) have been active in programs to improve employment opportunities for minorities, either through job, placement, or skills training. Firms participating in jobs have already created 105,000 permanent jobs and promised to provide at least 267,000 more for hard-core urban employment.[33]

Black Economic Development schemes and Black Capitalism was put in place to establish businesses within the existing economic community. Newly formed Black businesses are allowed to operate in a predominantly Black market.

---

[33] William L. Henderson and Larry C Ledebur, Government Incentives and Black Economic Development. Denison University.

CORE, the Black Muslims, and the Black Panthers help establish Black Capitalism. The A. Philip Randolph Institute and the NAACP have formulated programs to permit minorities to establish businesses within existing institutional frameworks.

The Biden-Harris Administration recently announced new actions to build Black wealth and "narrow the racial wealth gap." The administration is expanding access to two key wealth-creators—homeownership and small business ownership—in communities of color and disadvantaged communities.

The federal government's purchasing power to grow federal contracting with small, disadvantaged businesses by 50 percent has been sanctioned, translating to an additional $100 billion over five years and helping more minority Americans realize their entrepreneurial dreams.

Results

- Latina women and Latino men experienced the biggest gains in well-being, according to the American Human Development Index from Brooklyn, N.Y.-based nonprofit Social Science Research Council's Measure of America project. The index is a composite rating based on health, education, and income.[34]

- The Latino community's American Human Development Index scores increased 22 percent over the past 10 years versus just a 6.4 percent increase overall across the U.S.

- White men experienced the smallest improvement in well-being since 2008, aside from Native American men, who were the only group to experience a decline in their well-being.

- Black women made the second-largest gain in their well-being, with a 17.5 percent improvement.

- In other words, while more minorities are getting better opportunities, evidence suggests that inclusion is not working for everyone at the same rate.

_____

[34] http://www.measureofamerica.org/10yearsandcounting/

Quotas

The U.S. does not use the same direct quota system that India uses. Instead, they use a point system, under which candidates from historically disadvantaged groups such as Blacks or immigrants are given a few extra points in admission and appointment procedures. The U.S. also requires gender quotas on boards of directors. Arguments for increasing gender diversity on boards of directors by gender quotas range from ensuring equal opportunity to improving firm performance.

These quotas have both pros and cons. Quotas increase the number of women on boards of directors and the decision-making process is thought to improve with greater gender diversity on boards. Having female top executives positively affects women's career development at lower levels of an organization. However, quotas might imply that less experienced women will join boards because the supply of qualified women in senior executive positions is thin.

Progress

The good news is that Black Americans have progressed in education, business, housing, and quality of life in the U.S. There have been improvements across different areas such as Black employment and earnings since the 1960s, when many government tools were used to track racial disparities.

The unemployment gap between Black and white Americans is also decreasing. But we must ask, was that due to the inclusion of Black workers or the exclusion of white workers? Or was inclusion or exclusion even a factor?

We must also consider whether inclusion is even working for minorities. Despite the efforts, household wealth for Black Americans has remained flat while the white household wealth has steadily increased for thirty years.

In the process of answering that question, another arises. Are quotas inclusive of everyone? If the government was going to invest in small businesses and everybody was going to compete for that investment, that's one thing. However, the minute a portion of that investment is reserved "only for black-owned or female-owned businesses," by default the government is forcing the rest of the population to compete for the *remainder* and not the *whole*. Now, if the rest of the population has a bigger size and dimension that cannot fall under any quota, will that majority, or "unreserved," population feel excluded? It is likely they will because they have already been denied a slice of the pie. By introducing quotas, opportunities for the larger population have been decreased.

But the majority population is growing, be it US or India, and the laws of supply and demand dictate that if people's aspirations are growing along with their average educational qualifications and we cannot supply them with enough jobs or business opportunities, a resentment and feeling of exclusion will set in automatically. But if the equity being pushed includes a plan, like giving job security to everyone beyond any reservation, then such quotas *can* make sense in terms of overall inclusion. Perpetual reservations will not help; creating more opportunities will. The pie has to grow.

When we create those metrics and do not create more opportunities, many eligible people also feel excluded by default. Let's say the U.S. government has created quotas for women and for women of color. But many women do not want to be treated as a woman of color. My wife is one such woman. She thinks this designation insults her ability.

Hence, before hard demarcating quotas on certain metrics, all governments and organizations should consider who they are including and excluding by them. If we exclude more people in our attempts at inclusion, we are probably not helping much. We need to be relentless in pursuit of a process in which inclusion of a certain section will not lead to greater exclusion of another section but instead lead to making a wholly positive impact.

Perception of Success

In the efforts to include and measure success we often capture several metrics. But one element that trumps everything is the perception of success. For example, when asked specifically about the impact President Barack Obama has had on race relations in the U.S., a majority of Americans give the president credit for at least *trying* to make things better, but a quarter says he has made race relations worse. Some 51 percent of Black Americans say Obama has made progress toward improving race relations, and an additional 34 percent say he has tried but failed to make progress. Relatively few Black Americans (5 percent) say Obama has made race relations worse, while 9 percent say he has not addressed the issue at all. Among white Americans, 28 percent say Obama has made progress toward improving race relations and 24 percent say he has tried but failed to make progress. But a substantial share of white Americans (32 percent) say Obama has made race relations worse.

Perception is personal and, therefore, based upon opinion rather than fact. It is also often based on comparisons. If a frontline retail worker compares their income to a wealthy tech leader, they might perceive themselves as "poor" through that comparison. In addition, a difference in perception of equality exists. Black and white Americans disagree due to their perceptions. It leads one to wonder whether we will ever universally agree that equity has been reached.

Perception is the key. When the average quality of life of a majority population is not actually improving and there are more politically right schemes in place for minorities, without proper communication and proper engagement we create the perception that minority groups are getting everything good while majority groups are being deprived.

Fairness

The question of fairness illuminates the difference between equality and equity. Is it fair to include everyone at the same rate if equity is not present? For example, if we are forming a soccer team, do we prioritize a racial quota to form a diverse team, or are we looking for the best players? There is tension between including everyone and finding the best people for the job. Excluding someone because of their skin color, gender, or religion is unfair. However, isn't it unfair to exclude the most qualified just to meet quotas?

Next we must consider whether the efforts to include everyone harms the overall good of the community or country. When we funnel resources from the majority to the minority, sometimes the minority pool for a particular job in a specific context might not be as capable of delivering the results, and the success rate drops. That's what happens when lesser-qualified individuals are given opportunities.[35]

Feeling Discomfort

I shared my hesitation around this chapter and my thoughts about inclusion and exclusion with a very smart woman who was my boss in earlier life. She retired at fifty and kept busy golfing and doing other enjoyable things, but we keep in touch, share thoughts, and even go for lunch once in a while.

Her thoughts and opinions are usually very insightful and meaningful. In this instance, however, she surprised me a bit when she said, "It is okay if the majority is feeling uncomfortable. The discomfort is required for the change."

Knowing the rational person she is, I expected her to give me kudos for collecting the courage to discuss a majority perspective. It turns out it was more personal than that. In her very successful career as an entrepreneur and senior partner in one of the big Fours she always felt judged as a female. She has three awesome daughters, but based on her learned experience from early in her career she felt she could never talk about her kids and family at work. When her male counterparts talked about their kids there were no negative consequences, but when senior female leaders the same it was a reminder to

---

[35] This is an example and should not be taken as a general statement that all minority members are less qualified than majority members.

everyone around that they might not be available to go the extra mile and complete a complex assignment. They were always cast as the default caregiver for the kids—and hence, not as available as their male counterparts. In fear of missing out on the more challenging assignments, she decided to avoid talking about kids and family.

She is no pushover, but even with her top-notch capability and excellent personality, she felt outside of the boys' club. She shared their stories with a candor that hit me hard, and when she finished speaking, she paused. "Let them be uncomfortable for a bit," she repeated. "It is required."

I did not want to argue after that.

CONCLUSION

I have experienced inclusion from both sides. From personal experience, I can insist that we must find a balance between inclusion and exclusion. A portion of the majority are feeling uncomfortable. Inclusion is a change, and it is reality. Finding a balance will create the best performance environment that can be measured.

The efforts to include minorities are noble, but unless they are thoughtfully executed they can also create the possibility that majorities will be excluded. Blindly chasing equity metrics focused only on minority groups might include lesser qualified individuals being hired simply to fill a quota. If not done right (with a growth mindset), they also come in the form of limiting business opportunities for the majority of members. Initiatives to include minority groups should therefore focus on including majority groups along the journey. I was not joking when I suggested an employee resource group for the majority population should be a requirement. Like any ERG group, please make sure majority resource group has enough diverse participation to listen and understand the majority perspective.

KEY TAKEAWAYS

- Most initiatives, regulations, and quotas which have been put in place to pull up minority communities show progress in all fields for minorities.

- If overall growth is lacking, minority initiatives will be perceived to exclude the majority.

- When the average quality of life of a majority population is not actually improving and there are more politically right schemes in place for minorities, without proper communication and proper engagement we create the perception that minority groups are getting everything good while majority groups are being deprived.

- In India, the quota system led to a political dialogue that created a feeling of marginalization within the majority population. This pendulum effect occurs worldwide and needs to be addressed.

- Employee Resource Groups should include groups which focus on majority populations as much as minority populations.

CHAPTER 5:

EQUITY AS A PRINCIPLE

After spending some time on diversity and diverse thinking, I hope we all appreciate by now that diversity is broad and it is a reality. Our opinions about the topic matter little because diversity exists in almost everything in life. This means there are also global regulatory and social needs, and luckily, there are few ways to address them. One is to create a group within Human Resources or Environmental Social and Governance (ESG) to track, manage, improve and report required metrics and drive some actions reacting to regulatory needs. This requires treating diversity as a regulatory need and reacting to it as many organizations have done over the years as part of corporate social responsibility.

Since diversity is much broader than regulatory needs and is a more fundamental reflection of everything around us, the above approach might help us run our business but will not generate true value for the business or society. It will definitely not move the needle to the point where we can leave the world in a better place than how we found it.

So what is the alternative? Run more and more metrics and chase them? While measuring is a good start and there is nothing wrong with a small set of initial focus metrics, it is important to take a broader and more sustainable approach.

My recommendation is to adopt equity as a principle in whatever we do. When the time comes to decide between business outcomes, having established equity as an organization's principle or core value can easily help anyone in that organization arrive at the right decision with minimum ambiguity.

EQUITY AS A LIVED PRINCIPLE

I worked at a very large global company engaged in mining, manufacturing, retail and services, and they abide by the core value of *safety*. Ask anyone in the organization, from the CEO to the frontline staff, whether safety, production, or sales are more important, and the answer you get will be quick and consistent. It is "safety." *Safety* is that core value everyone lives up to and broadly shares without any hesitation, and it has been a core value for a while. But it took time for that value to truly sink in across the organization. It took effort by everyone, particularly the leaders at various levels, and it took reinforcement at every broadcast and conference. It took many emerging as role models and living the value. This example or similar such examples are important to understand as we talk about equity as a principle.

Equity will be a lived principle when, everyone within an organization can easily identify the need for equity when it arises—in *everything* they do—and are able to prioritize that need over speed or urgency with confidence and clarity.

Equity creates possibilities for most and creates the right balance of challenge and excitement. Typically humans are most engaged when they experience optimum challenge combined with line of sight to success. My now nine-year-old son is very competitive. He likes to race a lot. When he was even smaller, we used often go to the neighborhood soccer field and race from one post to the other side. He had tiny legs and lot of energy. We decided that I would start after he passed the center field. I did that because I cared about him and wanted him to have a fair chance. However once we made that calibration, I did not simply let him win every time to make him happy. Sometimes I won and sometimes he did. But what was more important was that we both enjoyed the races more and wanted to repeat the experience because it was challenging and interesting for both of us. More interestingly, as time passed and he got faster, my son insisted that I reduce his head start. Naturally, he wanted it to be more challenging for him. He does the same for me in swimming these days. He is a competitive swimmer and I am terrible at it. I get to go past the first flag before he starts. For me, that half soccer field or quarter swim length of equity makes it fun and fulfilling.

I believe the need for equity as a leveler in life and the positivity it generates is more obvious to and accepted by organizations than ever before.

As discussed in Chapter 4, diversity is usually broader than we think and potentially shows up in almost everything we do. As a result, equity also needs to be part or everything we do.

In other words, equity is not just the new thing a DEI department does. Far more than a Key Performance Indicator or a metric to employ, equity is a core principle that requires a uniform and uni-lateral application in every aspect of a business.

In this chapter, you see how equity is implemented in daily oper-ations such as hiring, pay scales, and access to selected facilities and suppliers. It is prevalent in internal and external communica-tions, mission statements, and everyday interactions. To employ equity effectively, each individual is valued in every situation for the value they provide. At the beginning and continuing through to the end of all operations, equity is a critical component for doing business well.

Starbucks

"We are on a journey to advance racial and social equity for our partners (employees), our community, and our society. And we have made progress. Almost 50 years ago, we set out to be a different kind of company—with a third-place community where everyone is welcome and respected at its core. But now, today, in this moment, we know there is much more to do. Bold actions that we must take as our journey continues to act with intention, transparency, and accountability.

It is a journey grounded in our mission to inspire and nurture the human spirit.

It is our responsibility, and it is our commitment."

Starbucks sees its customers as partners, which is why CEO Keven Johnston sent a letter on October 14, 2020, to clarify the organization's equity standards.

A few years prior, there had been an incident in a Philadelphia Starbucks. Two men entered the location to meet a friend. While they were waiting they decided to use the restroom, only to be denied by the manager. The problem arose when they asked why they were denied. The manager claimed they hadn't made a purchase, and the men countered by stating that others had not made a purchase and were given access. The event escalated, the police were called, and the men were arrested.[36]

This incident quickly became a public relations nightmare because the two men were Black. In a time with heightened sensitivities to racial injustice, this situation quickly went viral, drawing protesters who attempted to prevent the store from making any profits that day. The mayor released a statement and Starbucks quickly became

---

[36] The Guardian, April 16, 2018. https://www.theguardian.com/us-news/2018/apr/16/arrest-of-two-black-men-at-starbucks-for-trespassing-sparks-protests

a topic for corporate exclusion. Kevin Johnston had a corporate migraine on his hands—one that threatened the entire operation.

This incident prompted management to take the right actions and make equity a core value, a principle they would live by.

For Starbucks to resolve the situation and win the public relations battle, they had to act swiftly and with significant action.

Starbucks quickly announced that it would be "closing its more than 8,000 company-owned stores in the United States on the afternoon of May 29 to conduct racial-bias education geared toward preventing discrimination in our stores. The training will be provided to nearly 175,000 partners (employees) across the country, and will become part of the onboarding process for new partners."

Closing company-owned stores for inclusion training is a drastic action and elevated the importance of inclusion within the company and with stakeholders. With this bold move, Starbucks took the lead in addressing racial bias. Before the April 2018 incident, Starbucks had a DEI strategy. Post-incident, their strategy became supercharged, focused, and purposeful.

I have worked in large organizations with major heavy operations. I find a lots of parallel between equity and safety in large manufacturing organizations. Almost all heavy engineering-type organizations have a safety department and some safety metrics. Some stop there and focus on the optics and regulatory needs, whereas others, who make safety a priority above everything (including profit and production), turn the values from safety metrics to "Culture of Care." That's when it becomes real for their employees and other stakeholders.

Equity is similar. Most organizations now have a DEI strategy statement and maybe even a metric set they manage. The question is whether it is in the DNA of the organization and reflected in everything it does. When Starbucks made their bold move to close so many stores for DEI training, that was significant. An organization, especially one as large and public as Starbucks, must walk the talk. Equity must permeate the organization in all actions and activities.

Fortunately for Starbucks, the April 2018 incident led to significant change. When the streets of America erupted with chants of "Black Lives Matter" in June 2020, Starbucks stepped forward and announced it would donate $1 million to support racial justice-oriented causes.[37] But there was still more work to do. The company faced criticism yet again when an internal order was exposed that banned Starbucks employees from wearing any merchandise supporting Black Lives Matter.[38] They subsequently reversed the policy, going so far as to distribute Black Lives Matter T-shirts to their baristas.[39]

By the time Johnston sent his October 14th, 2020 letter, Starbucks committed to embrace DEI fully. This could not become just another slogan but rather had to become part of the fabric of the corporation. DEI would become central to their mission, beginning with executives, creating a "Third Place" where everyone was welcome. They would set high standards and hold themselves accountable. A few months later, in January 2021, Starbucks announced it would be launching the Starbucks Community Resiliency Fund with a $100 million endowment to support equity and inclusion in the communities it serves.[40]

To ask whether Starbucks would have taken this stand without the 2018 incident in Philadelphia is moot. The idealists like to believe companies do what is right without being forced. However, there is no doubt that some corporate leaders are genuinely moved and feel compelled to confront bias, beginning with themselves. In the end, Starbucks did the right thing. That is all that matters.

---

[37] Foxbusiness.com, June 2, 2020.

[38] USAToday.com, June 11, 2020.

[39] WallStreetJournal.com, June 12, 2020.

[40] Stories.starbucks.com, June 12, 2021.

The world is too connected and live all the time. That's why it is more important than ever before to walk the talk if trust with stakeholders to be retained.

Google

The technology industry in North America has long been known for being dominated by white men, particularly in technical jobs. At Google, Black women represent only 0.7 percent of its technical workforce, and Black employees make up 2.4 percent of the technical workforce overall, according to the company's 2020 diversity report. At Facebook, Black employees make up only 1.7 percent of its tech workforce, the diversity report said.[41]

Dr. Timnit Gebru arrived at Google with a long history of groundbreaking research, insightful innovation, and racial activism. She worked for Apple from 2004-2017, developing signal-processing algorithms for the iPad. She then joined Fei-Fei Li's lab at Stanford, where she combined deep learning with Google Street View to estimate the demographics of neighborhoods. The project was widely acclaimed by many news organizations. When she joined Microsoft in 2017, she mentioned how she was one of only a few black researchers in the tech industry. By the time she was hired in 2018 as the technical co-lead of Google's Ethical Artificial Intelligence Team, she had built a strong resume of technology innovation and a reputation as someone who was not afraid to stand for ethical standards. After being encouraged to explore the downside of Google's A.I. technology, she completed her research and compiled her findings into a paper, which sailed through an internal review. She then submitted the paper to a prominent conference, where it was accepted.

However, according to media and her statements, Gebru then met unexpected resistance from the person who encouraged the research. He demanded she withdraw the paper, or at least remove

---

[41] EEOC.gov

her name and all of the other Google employees connected to it. He released a message claiming she had resigned despite her willingness to negotiate.[42]

By itself, this action was egregious enough, but when a diversity recruiter was terminated shortly after, the story became headline news that would become a PR nightmare for Google.

Christina Curley was hired in 2014 in part to recruit candidates from historically Black colleges. The creation of that position sent positive signals to the world, especially since Google was not known for making those specific hires at that time. Within six years, she had hired 300 engineers from historically black colleges.

Then, in a surprising move, she was terminated. In a series of tweets, she tells how she was

- denied multiple promotions,
- put on performance improvement plans,
- subjected to reduced compensation,
- yelled at,
- excluded from meetings,
- denied leadership roles,
- harassed by managers,
- told her that her Baltimore accent was a disability she needed to disclose to colleagues.[43]

There is always more to the story than what is in social media, but it seems obvious that the end of this story was not what Google or Christina would have wanted it to be. When I talk about this with folks in industry, I see some interestingly polarized reactions. Some quickly get angry about the employer; others feel sorry for the employee. While I appreciate both reactions, I wonder about the

---

[42] Wired, June 2021.

[43] twitter.com

difficulty of living equity as a principle, when the best and brightest in industry get into such regretful situations?

To be clear, I am not criticizing Google or Starbucks by discussing them here. I can't remember of a day when my wife and/or I have not been to a Starbucks. Even my nine-year-old has his favorite beverage (steamed milk with a shot of vanilla). Besides drinks and snacks, it's a place I got to for alone time to write, read, and reflect. My family and I love the brand, and we feel the same about Google. My son has asked me several times how we found things if there was no Google when we were growing up. Even now, I am not sure if I know how to survive without Google on my phone and in my life. Instead of criticism, I offer an acknowledgment: the equity journey can be curvy and difficult, even for those on top.

Although it is obvious that this journey is not easy one, failing to create a truly inclusive and equitable environment for all members, staff, and candidates is proven to be bad business.

Boeing

Boeing has made DEI a conscious decision in everything they do, from hiring veterans to make up 15 percent of their workforce to ensuring zero workplace injuries, giving financial support for employee education, running training programs for all employees at every level, and protecting the human rights of every employee (including through products and environment safety). As seen in their DEI statement below, their organization-wide approach to equity aims to provide equality to every employee in every field.

> *Each member of our global team brings something uniquely valuable to Boeing, and we grow stronger when everyone has an opportunity to contribute. We continue to take meaningful steps to advance an open and respectful environment where everyone feels welcome, not just at Boeing, but also in the surrounding communities where we live. Boeing's culture of*

care involves creating an environment that retains and attracts the world's top talent and inspires every teammate to do their best work and grow their careers while making a positive impact on the world.

Their website touts the stories of Native American, Asian American, Black, Hispanic, and women workers throughout Boeing's many divisions.[44] In their 2021 Workforce Diversity Report, they revealed

22.9 percent of the company's workforce are women, including nearly one in three (31.8 percent) executives and over one in five (22.2 percent) managers.

- Asian Americans are significantly more represented in the Boeing workforce than in the general population (14.2 percent versus 5.4 percent). They are statistically over-represented among executives (8.3 percent), managers (7.9 percent), engineers (17.6 percent), and production workers (16.6 percent). Asian Americans are also 13.9 percent of new hires.
- Black employees represent 6.4 percent of the workforce, and Latino employees are 7.0 percent.
- African Americans who are executives (6.5 percent) and managers (6.0 percent) are consistent with the overall workforce but fall to 4.4 percent for engineers and rise to 7.6 percent for production/maintenance workers. The percentage of Black executive council members, the top internal management body, is an unusually high at 25 percent. Meanwhile, 8.3 percent of board members are Black.

These numbers show that Boeing is walking the inclusion talk. Two conclusions can be drawn from the above stories. First, to achieve goals for DEI, it is essential to incorporate equity as a principle in everything an organization does. Second, equity must be at the core of any successful DEI journey.

---

[44] Boeing.com

Stand-alone policies of equity fail miserably. This practice is tantamount to saying one thing and practicing another. Instead, equity must be a part of an organization's core value, a principle followed in conducting every aspect of the company's business. Equity cannot simply be handed off to human resources to enforce. If so, it will remain just another hot topic that a department perceives as its function. It might become the pet project or responsibility of one or two people. That is the sure way to ensure Equity measures fail. Instead, Equity must be a priority, a stated value, and part of strategy, woven into the action plan by being reinforced throughout the culture. The principle of equity needs to be embedded in the organizational culture and should be reflected in everything the organization does, from hiring a new employee or worker to termination or retirement. Equity must be embraced and enforced in every department, from accounting, manufacturing, sales, or marketing to employee benefits.

VIEWS OF EQUITY

To bring in this holistic approach, many organizations are conducting "Organizational Equity Audits." Organizational Equity is defined as the relative distribution of power and resources among key internal organizational stakeholders, including directors, executives, managers, and employees. Importantly, an analysis or audit of this equity considers the already unequal social distribution of equity and is especially focused on the experiences of individuals from traditionally under-resourced and underrepresented groups.

An organizational equity audit involves processing and collecting data related to the relative power and workplace experiences of individuals in disadvantaged groups. This data is then used to identify the causes of inequitable influence and resource distribution. Once the audit process is completed, it is imperative that organizational leaders take action to remedy all inequities discovered. Included in the audit, leaders collect data about organizational systems, employee backgrounds, and contemporary social systems.

This data is valuable for interpreting information related to employee recruitment, hiring, retention and advancement, employee pay and benefits, employee experiences, engagement and satisfaction, leadership prioritization, and resource commitment.

Without regular monitoring in these areas, organizational leaders may miss early indicators of organizational inequity and, as a result, be left clueless as to why they fail to diversify their leadership team, appeal to young workers, or receive public backlash when they fail to meet their professed commitments to diversity and inclusion. By quickly addressing issues related to organizational inequity, companies nurture an environment that meets the needs of all employees and reap external and internal benefits.

Stephanie Mahin, Ph.D., and Shoshana Rosenberg, J.D., MBA, FIP, PLS, CIPP, CIPM, write, "U.S. leaders must keep a keen eye on their organization's internal equity. With frequent, careful audits, organizations can intelligently and strategically begin making the interventions necessary for true equity. As they achieve equity, these organizations will see numerous rewards and be more likely to outperform their peers, have more engaged and committed employees, and know they are on a journey toward creating a culture people can believe in. In other words, leaders who consider Equity and Inclusion a strategic part of their culture enjoy a higher ROI. Isn't that what any good business leader wants? A companywide commitment to DEI makes for the best business that earns the best profits."

CONCLUSION

> Equity is a core value, not for just one or two metrics. For example, Canada is a nation with a rich indigenous history. Unfortunately, that history is riddled with inequity. To ensure fairness and balance going forward, leaders must look beyond a single metric to ensure Equity is a central principle. It must become a principle in hiring for government jobs and encourage hiring in all private businesses. It must

become a principle to create some position of advantage, preference, or focus for recruiting the indigenous population in various posts, especially in leadership, management, and executive positions. The playing field must be level and fair. Minority candidates should be given a chance to compete for open positions. The process must be applied through-out the recruitment and development processes. DEI must be reinforced in every formal and informal communication, reflecting its priority as an anchor in their culture. It cannot be relegated to a policy, poster, or particular department. If any organization follows equity as a principle, it will automat-ically flow through all the functions.

KEY TAKEAWAYS

- Equity as a principle needs to be practiced by any organi-zation in a holistic way.
- Metrics are important as a starting point and measurement.
- A handful of metrics *only* will not move the needle.
- Dimensions of diversity are too broad to list and measure everything.
- Frequent equity audits and revisiting early indicators can be a very effective way to progress the journey.

CHAPTER 6:

INCLUSION IS A CHOICE

*C*hapter 6 steers us into the land of frightening, strategic choices. Inclusion isn't an accident but a choice that we consciously make. The decision to become more inclusive is often threatening and leads us into unfamiliar and often terrifying territory. So we take it slow, inching along, playing it safe. But is playing it safe the best business practice? In this chapter, you will learn how inclusion without clarity can be paralyzing and that almost nothing big can be achieved without an engaged team. To create that high-performing team, we must combine psychological safety with inclusion.

Teamwork

According to several studies on personality, there is a correlation between fast, action-driven work and an extreme sense of accountability. If an individual contributor gets the work done very fast, it feels great because, one assumes, they have a high sense of accountability and are driven by action. About two decades ago, however, I learned that strategy might be great for an individual performer, but not as helpful when trying to grow as a leader.

Any significant success or outcome usually requires teamwork. More often than not, it requires cross functional teams to come together. Nothing big can be accomplished by one individual. No matter how talented or charismatic, a leader needs the entire team and more to be successful. We are not technically correct when we say Elon Musk created Tesla, Bill Gates discovered Windows, or Steve Jobs invented the iPhone. Instead, we must acknowledge that there is always a big team of very smart and dedicated people working to make big things happen.

There has been a large body of research published in the last decade or so which clearly indicates the best performing teams enjoy high levels of psychological safety as part of their culture. There are many accurate and detailed definitions of psychological safety from experts. Often, psychological safety is defined as one's belief that they won't be punished or humiliated for speaking up with ideas, questions, concerns, or mistakes. Harvard organizational behavioral scientist Amy Edmondson first introduced the construct of "team psychological safety" and defined it as "a shared belief held by members of a team that the team is safe for interpersonal risk taking." To me, psychological safety is achieved when no one holds back questions, suggestions, or critiques and everyone shares all of the above in a respectful manner.

So: we need engaged, large, cross-functional teams to achieve material outcomes. Teams perform best when the phycological safety quotient is high. With those two givens, where does inclusion fit?

Inclusion is the choice which engages people with diverse backgrounds in a psychologically safe and equitable manner.

Remember, diversity is reality and it is truly powerful. When, through the choice of inclusion, we create an equitable platform combined with psychological safety, high-performing teams are instantly created.

But if all that is true, it is difficult to understand where the problem lies. Why doesn't every organization and leader put their highest focus on inclusion and reap its rewards? Simply put, it is much harder than it seems. The difficulties themselves are not easy to unravel. First, including diversity is new and sometimes may be uncomfortable. Second, it can be equally uncomfortable to be included. Finally, inclusion takes effort and time and can often feel like a decelerator.

Including Diversity: unknown and uncomfortable

Early in my career, I was setting up a data and analytics team for a large healthcare product. I had been a people leader for only a couple of years at that time. We used Crystal Reports, Microsoft SQL, and some ORACLE. I needed to set up a team with about ten Crystal Report developers and about ten or so database administrators and stored procedure programmers, but had a short window of time in which to do so. We had already signed the contract. Any delay in onboarding my team meant a loss of revenue and, potentially, a loss of the contract.

I decided to assemble a team of members with varied levels of experience and found myself hiring some folks with 1-2 years of post-graduate experience in those technical skill areas and some with about 5-10 years. Around that time my boss referred me to the résumé of a Database Administrator (DBA) with more than 25 years of experience. Simple math told me the candidate was about fifteen years older than me at the time. With my limited people leadership experience, I had never overseen anyone who was more than few years older than me.

I still remember that interview today. I am not sure who was more uncomfortable—me or the candidate. The strangest part was that I could not locate the source of my discomfort. From a technical perspective, I was clear and confident; I knew what I was looking for. Neither I was threatened by his experience. And yet, discomfort lingered.

In my attempts at introspection and understanding, I thought of that discomfort quite a bit. Now I think it came from the thought of directing and managing someone so much older than me. The candidate was a person from another generation, different from me and rest of the team in few ways. Besides being older, he had a different level of clarity and expectations regarding his work/life balance. He had needs and obligations that meant he had to leave right around five (unlike most of us single professionals who liked to hang out for longer hours after work, sometimes even get a drink or whatnot).

As they say, you only grow when you are uncomfortable. I learned a lot from that experience. I did offer him the job, as he clearly had more technical experience than anyone in the newly formed team. And, after about three months, I learned to see beyond his demographic. I began to appreciate his family commitments in the evening and to appreciate him as a human, not just a DBA. When my perspective shifted, I moved most team events and celebrations to the lunch instead of dinner hour to respect his evening commitments.

In one winter outdoor team event, we decided to invite my team along with family and/or significant others. That was first event I hosted as a leader which included people other than my employees themselves. I learned that something very powerful that day, and it has stayed with me ever since: if you really care about knowing your colleagues, you always need to know them beyond work. You need to connect as humans. To connect with whole self of a person you almost naturally have to connect with their loved ones as well. From my personal experience, every time I got to connect with someone in that holistic way, I immediately felt that trust went up and so did engagement. Of course, there is a line between work and home, and there can be downsides if we inadvertently make an intrusion into an employee's personal life. I talk about this in *Leadership 4.0*. Here I will only say human connection is beautiful and it can be very powerful without crossing privacy lines.

As time passed, other DBAs in the team began seeking out their older team member for technical mentoring and guidance when any complicated issues arose. I took advantage of that, too, and would sometime leverage his experience. Those experiences made another deep impression on me: there is always something to learn from everyone around me, even if they report to me. I believe and practice that perspective every day. I have a fantastic team; each and every member teaches me something new every day.

As you know by now, age is not the only diversity apparent in the workforce. Recall the many diversity dimensions we talked about in Chapter 3. How many have you directly experienced? Do you have someone in your team who needs to use a wheelchair to come to work? Do you have someone in your team who is undergoing gender transition? If not, you are not the only one. The workforce is still learning how to create an equitable environment that includes diversities in a productive, comfortable way that will allow the leader and employee to feel comfortable navigating the new and the unknown.

The key is to believe in the goodness of the outcome and approach each diversity with an open mind. Easier said than done. But remember discomfort often means growth, and that you will learn something new as well.

Being Included Can Be uncomfortable, Too

I mentioned earlier that I am considered a "visible minority," though I do not feel that way at all anymore. I actually forget about my minority attributes unless I am required to fill out a Stats Canada or government form that asks about them. It was not like that for me when I first started working in North America.

I was in Philadelphia at the time. I remember when Susan (name changed), the head of the healthcare business unit in which I worked, invited me to her house for a barbeque on a Saturday afternoon. I was not sure I wanted to attend, but I had nothing else to do that day and it would have been impolite not to be there. So I decided to go.

The visit was full of awkward moments. First, everyone but me showed up with a drink or something to share. I came with nothing. I had no clue about what the norm was; I had no idea that bringing something was what everyone did. (In my defense, these were the pre-Google, early internet days and we only had Nokia phones.)

The second awkward moment occurred when I noticed that the food consisted of beef patties, buns, and salad. Though I do not have any dietary restrictions around beef, it is not my favorite. But my usual go to-meat choices, chicken and fish, were not on the menu, so I managed with what was there and did my best not to express any dislike.

Finally, after the barbeque, folks there decided to go trap shooting. Until then, the only thing I had ever shot was an air balloon at a carnival—nothing like the real, big guns with significant recoil I encountered that afternoon. And while I did eventually enjoy myself—so much so that Susan's husband invited me to join them on a proper hunting trip—I experienced a lot of anxiety until I got going.

That afternoon, with its awkwardness and enjoyments, left yet another lesson. Susan and her family went above and beyond to include me and make my afternoon as meaningful and enjoyable as theirs. And yet, my own discomfort and hesitation at being included held me back in many ways. Yes, I eventually opened up as the afternoon progressed and yes, we are still connected friends several years later. But the point is that *being included* can be as difficult as *including*. Like most things in life, it is a two-way street. It is not only about majority groups including the diverse folks, it also about minority groups walking the path of discomfort in an effort to engage.

Today, almost all of my close friends have a different skin color than me. I can't see that difference any more, but I can see that I have some of the best friends one can hope for in life. Many of them I work with, or have worked with in the past. But I did walk the path of learning and discomfort that leads to fulfillment.

Deceleration and Speed

There is an African proverb I like a lot. It says, "If you want to go fast, go alone. If you want to go far, go together."

Once I started working for large organization after exiting my startup, I went through the annual appraisal cycles the employees of most large organizations go through. Through those performance cycles, 360 reviews, and other feedback mechanisms, I always heard a few consistent praises and reinforcements. My reviewers were overwhelmingly positive about my ability to take on a huge workload, juggle multiple projects, never drop the ball, rapidly deliver assignments, effectively work with everyone, and, most importantly, decide and think fast on most problem statements or opportunity statements that were thrown at me. Over the years I noticed a theme: fast and a lot. Since it was mostly through consulting fast and "a lot" that my skills usually translated to revenue and profitability, I kept going faster and bigger. Year after year, organization after organization, I continued to be a top-rated employee—without exception. I dominated whatever scale the organization had. Obviously, it felt good.

It also felt good that I have loved all my people leaders over the years. Each and every one are now my personal friends; I consider them family. One passed away during the pandemic and it shocked my system. I could not stop thinking of our first lunch together and how he was hyper focused on achieving a good folder structure before we started our project. That is a thing I have done ever since, even today. At the beginning of a piece of work, I first get the shell and structure in place, then fill the content and adjust.

I was constantly encouraged to be fast and high-performing, I kept doing more and more. When I became first line leader, I tried to hire people who could replicate that at scale and started building what I thought of as "high performing" teams. Success came to the team and we were all happy.

That is, we were happy until I was thrown into a very unknown technology and domain: backfilling some massive attrition in that very project. Here I am going to date myself. It was a JD Edwards-based project for very large printer company. I knew a bit of IBM AS400 technology and had done some RPG 400 programming prior to that, but what I knew was not expertise and it was nowhere good enough to lead a JDE major enhancement project.

My knowledge simply was not adequate to drive the functional and technical decisions, so I took on accountability for the deliverables and lead the team from a managerial and people leadership perspective. There were two senior experts in the team and rest were learning. The key functional specialist was an introverted individual, knowledgeable but very submissive and with a quiet personality.

As you can probably imagine, I felt a lot of discomfort. My pace of decision making was challenged, my ability to lead by example was limited. It was time for me to slow down and align with the pace of my expert functional specialist. It was my responsibility to create an environment in which someone much quieter and more introverted than me and rest of the team could make design decisions so that we could all be successful. And at the end, after many long nights and weekends after weekends, it *was* a very successful project. But the slow pace and my inability to move quickly, at the pace I'd grown comfortable with, was very uncomfortable for me for months.

But it taught me some valuable things my previous leaders had never told me. The metric of success for a true leader is not how fast they progress or how many decisions they make. Rather, it is in how many decisions are made by the team *without much help from the leader*. And it is not always about doing many, many things at the same time, but instead getting the most important thing done with quality. Finally, it is most important to create space for everyone on the team to engage and contribute. There will be and always have been people who are not comfortable standing up and communicating their opinion. There will be always those who speak most in the discussions. The task of the leader is to create multiple channels and meet people where they are most comfortable to get the most out of everyone. Inclusion delivered value, but I was not able to see that in the beginning and the outcome was slower than my usual.

Inclusion is a deliberate choice and needs to be purposeful. Here is an example. Let's say the business development group is working on a confidential M&A transaction. In those circumstances it is normal, for good business reasons, to start with a small group of people who are authorized by a special confidential agreement to work on the transaction without including everyone in the organization. On the other hand, when we want to understand employee perspectives on culture, or things of that nature, it is normal to survey and reach out to everyone in the organization.

When we include lots of people without purpose, it does not engage them and the result is intellectual tourism. It takes a longer time and it's not productive for anyone. On the other side of the spectrum, choosing not to include the right stakeholders and to make unilateral decisions might feel faster and more efficient, but we are missing out on the diverse opinions needed to make complex decisions. It is like when I was an individual contributor. As soon as I wanted to scale as a leader, it failed. I needed the cognitive power of the entire team.

The Best Leader With The Best Results

While inclusion might feel alien and cumbersome at the beginning, the leader who knows the lessons includes the right stakeholders in the appropriate time, place, and manner and becomes the best leader delivering the best results. It is not just about producing a product. 'How' is as important. If the 'How' is right, it creates sustainable pace for future. There is considerable joy in seeing team members develop their skills and achieve success along the way. I found immense satisfaction from seeing them engage and take initiative. Inclusion should not feel slow but rather valuable.

Over the years, I realized:

- Inclusion is a fine balance between intellectual tourism and do-it-yourself.
- Inclusion without clarity can be paralyzing.
- Inclusion without psychological safety is useless.
- Inclusion provides everyone with required access to opportunities and resources.
- Inclusion efforts in the workplace help to give traditionally marginalized groups, like those based on gender, race, or even those with physical or mental disabilities, a means to feel equal in the workplace.

INCLUSION

Therefore, inclusion is a valuable organizational tool. When used effectively, inclusion ensures that all employees have access to all services and positions, regardless of age, gender, origin, sexual orientation, or health status. All diversities should be able to integrate into the company.

But there is a significant difference between *inclusion* and *integration*. Just as we differentiated equality from equity earlier, we must also draw a fine line between these two important concepts. With *integration*, an individual must make an adjustment to the system and make the effort to integrate and normalize. Meanwhile, the principle of *inclusion* modifies the modes of operation and accommodation in a way so they can integrate effortlessly and work under good conditions.

While integration is more of a transaction, inclusion is a transformation. Integration rearranges the chairs, so everyone has a place to sit. Inclusion, however, values each person sitting in those chairs. Inclusion transforms society, aiming to overcome all accessibility barriers in traditional structures (leisure, health, employment, education, social services, etc.). An inclusive company is one in which the transformation of inclusion is embedded in how it operates.

6 Characteristics of Workplace Inclusion

Deloitte (2018) articulates six characteristics that make a workplace inclusive:

1. Commitment – personally and professionally dedicate to inclusivity.
2. Courage – humble about their own limitations.
3. Cognizance – conscious of their own blind spots.
4. Curiosity – open-minded.
5. Cultural Intelligence – attentive to other cultures.
6. Collaboration – empower others to think and flourish.

Here are a few practical steps to take to develop your team.

- Establish participative decision-making. Encourage a broad set of ideas and input from all colleagues.
- Build strong teams by fostering trust and encouraging healthy conflict among team members to build bonds.
- Ensure impartial treatment by treating all employees fairly when allocating resources and making decisions.
- Take the time to train everyone in the proper usage of decision-making systems. This is particularly important when the approach is data-backed. Use the data to ensure leaders are positioned to shape positive perceptions of workplace inclusion.

An interesting side of inclusion could be leading to intellectual curiosity. I love this term because it fosters curiosity and cultural intelligence. We all learn and grow when we care enough to ask and listen. But more than that, it boosts psychological safety so everyone wants to engage.

Implementing Inclusion

Choose inclusion deliberately. If not done appropriately, inclusion could lead to many problems. For example, if you use inclusion as a consent-driven tactic, you can be paralyzed and never take the necessary action. There are always more people to ask and listen to. After all, many people love offering an opinion. When discussing a new project, they will often begin with, "I am concerned about ..." That is not productive leadership.

Another problem rests at the other end of the spectrum where exclusion lies. We discussed earlier how it might be faster and easier simply to decide for yourself. But then, that isn't inclusion, is it? The challenge is to find the right balance of inclusion. We also mentioned earlier that inclusion brings in the right people at the right levels. Not everyone is included in every decision, and that requires some exclusion. Find that balance between intellectual tourism and exclusion. Goodness is found somewhere in the middle. That's why identifying the appropriate level of inclusion is extremely important.

I think the easiest way to think about inclusion is as a choice. Defining and prioritizing inclusion is a conscious choice made based on two criteria. First, we look at the situation, and second, by asking about the appropriate level of inclusion. We choose who to include at what time and for what reason based on the task at hand. To become inclusive leaders, we make the decision that leads to the best results.

Inclusion and Psychological Safety

When you include people appropriately, you create a psychologically safe space for them to contribute. It is not so much their declared gender or physical ability or any other specific box you can check on a form. But rather, inclusion is the choice you can make to create the best environment where everyone delivers their best and makes the organization operate at its peak performance. That environment delivers the ultimate profit because it is psychologically safe and each can contribute without fear.

Unfortunately, I have seen some leaders having hard time listening and they are so obsessed about speaking. I have been in breakout sessions in diversity and inclusion workshops where I saw people from majority groups being very careful and speaking and sharing their opinion, but not making the same effort to listen.

But once, I was in a board strategy session where we were deliberating about a brand-new EDI strategy for the organization. The idea was for the board members to break out into groups of three or so, discuss for thirty minutes, and come back for group sharing. Two other gentlemen I know and respect were in my group. They are both very well-read and well-spoken. I could feel the silence in our group around speaking on the topic at hand, almost as if my groupmates felt the need to hold back and let me decide the direction of the discussion. I appreciated that, in the moment, but later followed up with one of the gentlemen to asked whether he was worried about saying something which might somehow offend me as a minority. He gave me an honest answer. He said that he struggles with the line on this topic and is always extra careful to not come across as exclusive.

As I mentioned before, the choice of inclusion should not only be limited to visible minority participation. It should create an environment in which majority groups feel safe and included as well.

Organizations must appreciate the diversity of perspectives, ideas, and methods while employing equity as a principle. Inclusion is a choice. Finding the appropriate level of inclusion is also a choice, as is creating a psychologically safe environment in which everybody can contribute.

When equity is established as valued principle and inclusion is practiced, good things happen within the organization. People engage when they feel safe and valuable because they believe they have a fair chance to progress and prove their abilities within the organization. Without this psychological safety, they disengage and either leave the organization or "quietly quit," staying but doing the minimum to stay employed.

Once employees feel safe and confident of fair play, they are encouraged to seize opportunities to engage at a higher level. Psychological safety is a key component in creating a successful and productive team. Google found that *team psychological safety* led to the most effective team production, how to leverage data, and key attributes of a most effective and productive team. According to Forbes Business Council, "establishing a culture that promotes psychological safety is the first step in making employees feel welcome to share their ideas. In a safe environment, employees have no fear of being ridiculed or facing professional sanctions for their statements."

What is the ROI of psychological safety?

- Employees feel safe and comfortable.
- Psychological safety improves employee performance by allowing more creativity and innovation since employees feel safe to voice new ideas.
- Psychological safety also increases employees' commitment to their organization, increasing employee retention.
- Communication, engagement, and knowledge sharing improve when psychological safety is present in the workplace. Employees tend to become more open to learning, including learning from failure, since their failures are not held against them.
- Employees also have more positive attitudes in the workplace and higher initiative levels.
- Employees become more open-minded, resilient, motivated, and persistent when they feel safe, therefore improving their performance.[45]

If I am asked today what my number one priority as a leader is, my answer is simple. It to assemble the right team and create a psychologically safe space for them to accomplish their objectives.

---

[45] Hutchison, J. (2020, April 8). Psychological safety and transparent communication at work: Strengthening collaboration and innovation [Video].

Spectrum of Inclusion vs Engagement

Earlier, we discussed finding the right balance based on the situation. To do so, we need to understand how to find the balance between including everyone and making unilateral decisions.

Moving beyond integration to establish a robust diversity with an inclusion strategy requires a commitment to curiosity, cultural intelligence, and collaborative success.

So, what does it take to build a successful inclusion strategy? At a high level, McKinsey recommends that top-performing companies implement the following four imperatives:

Start at the top, where all cultural changes begin. Without a commitment from the C-suite, there will be no sustained improvement. The CEO needs to make the conscious choice and commit to adopting equity as a principle and framing inclusion as a choice. Galvanize the organization around these principles and choices. Use them as pillars to fuel the strategic success of the organization. Then galvanize the entire organization, beginning with the upper managers and working through each level. Everyone is important, so every level must receive training and attention. The middle managers are critical because they promote ownership of their core businesses, encourage role modeling, hold their executives and managers to account, and ensure efforts are sufficiently resourced and supported centrally.

Next, define inclusion and diversity priorities based on the business-growth strategy's drivers. Top-performing companies invest in internal research to understand which specific strategies best support their business-growth priorities. Such strategies include attracting and retaining the right talent and strengthening decision-making capabilities. Leading companies also identify the mix of inherent traits (such as gender, ethnicity, etc.) and acquired traits (such as educational background, specific training, and experience) that are most relevant for their organization, using advanced business and people analytics. Language is important. Be careful to carefully explain the differences between equality and equity, inclusion, and integration.

Third, craft a targeted portfolio of inclusion and diversity policies and practices to transform the organization. The best companies use targeted thinking to prioritize the I&D initiatives in which they invest, ensuring alignment with the overall growth strategy. They recognize the necessity of building an inclusive organizational culture and use a combination of "hard" and "soft" wiring to create a coherent narrative and program that resonates with employees and stakeholders, helping drive sustainable change.

Finally, tailor the strategy to maximize local impact. Top and rapidly improving companies recognize the need to adapt their approach to three specific areas. First, they adapt to different parts of the business. DEI is important to sales and marketing, research and development, manufacturing, and human resources. Next, DEI is important to all locations, not just the headquarters. Lastly, DEI is critical to every sociocultural context. It is not just to make "them" happy but to benefit everyone.[46]

Inclusion Paralysis

While implementing these four steps, I need to remind you of the pesky problem of *inclusion paralysis*. Inclusion is the proven practice of bringing the best ideas forward from the most engaged teams. However, tipping too far into the inclusion spectrum can lead to inaction.

Sometimes we are so well-meaning that we become bogged down trying to please everyone. Inclusion paralysis results when we ask, "How do you get anything done when everyone has a say in everything?" This is one of the myths of what a democratic organization is and how it functions. The dreaded scenario that gets conjured up is some variety of complete and utter chaos, with everyone speaking at once and nothing actually happening. The simplistic

---

[46] McKinsey & Company.

alternative option is to dismiss involvement completely. Unfortunately, businesses and organizations have spent several decades trying the second option, and the result has been decreased productivity, missed innovation, and human beings showing up to work half-present and holding back most of their skills, capabilities, and intelligence for fear it would not be heard anyway.

CONCLUSION

Building a fearless, inclusive organization that realizes the benefits of diversity through greater inclusion and belonging is the most important goal for any leader today. That holds for both the public and private sectors. Leaders who care about diversity and inclusion must care about psychological safety, just as those who care about psychological safety must also care about diversity, inclusion, and belonging. Inclusion needs to be purposeful and deliberate. Inclusion without purpose can be paralyzing and disengaging.

KEY TAKEAWAYS

- Choice of inclusion is a very important tool.
- It modifies the modes of operation and accommodation in a profound way so that each person can integrate effortlessly and work under good conditions.
- Inclusion comes with its challenges and can lead to inclusion paralysis unless it is deliberate and purpose driven.

CHAPTER 7:

AWARENESS and ACCEPTANCE FRAMEWORK

To this point in the journey, we have discussed the need for and the value of DEI. Some, like Starbucks, have stepped into the leadership role, while others are work in progress and some still do resist. Wherever you are in your journey, it is time to become aware, accept, and change outdated beliefs; the world does not depend on them and will look more and more diverse regardless. To me, most things begin with awareness and understanding. In this chapter, I will talk about a framework which we will later use for assessing and measuring progress through the journey.

To change our beliefs, we must step back and analyze the process of how we have come to establish them. Let's start with understanding a simple awareness, acceptance, and belief journey. The first part of this chapter details this process. The second part presents a 2x2 grid that is a framework for measuring levels of awareness and acceptance. I created the 2x2 grid based on my personal experience, as well as formal and informal interviews with other leaders from industry and academia. The framework can be applied easily

Awareness-Acceptance-Belief

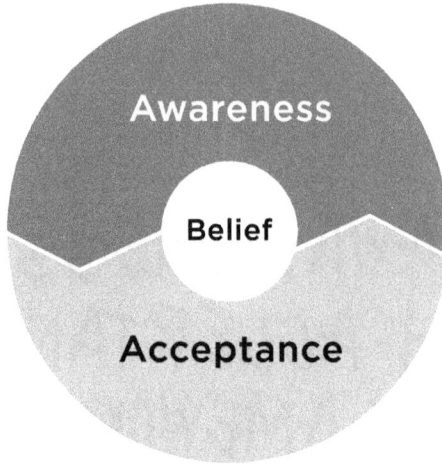

to your organization to help identify your level of awareness and acceptance. In the process, you will have more clarity about what you believe and how you can change those beliefs to more inclusive and productive ones. This 2x2 framework is also useful for individual professionals if you simply want to assess yourself as a professional on the grid.

AWARENESS

Any type of problem-solving or process improvement begins with awareness. If you are unaware of the problem and possibilities, there is no compelling reason for understanding and even less of a reason to change. Too many of us are stuck in this static state, holding fast to what we learned were "best practices" even when all signs indicate they are slipping into obsolescence.

Best Practices is an interesting concept. The concept can be useful if relevant. So many times I see consulting organizations that are stuck to older best practices and applying them to their clients' problems year after year without any tangible, trackable results. My caution would be to never trust *best practices* without verification.

Unawareness can be deliberate or neglectful, leading to a blind, negligent unconscious sense of false enlightenment. When we are unaware, we delude ourselves into believing there are no pressing problems when in reality our foundations of belief are crumbling. In such situations we are headed for irrelevance but believe we are on the right path.

However, when we are aware of what we believe, we can measure our beliefs against the facts and reality of the situation. From there, we can measure our level of acceptance and determine whether our beliefs are inclusive or not, productive or not. That process holds the potential for productive change, which is critical for any journey.

Awareness is defined as "informed; alert; knowledgeable; sophisticated."[47] To be aware also means continually monitoring the changing situation. We must be alert and actively observant of the who, what, when, where, why, and how individuals and groups interact. For example, we need to be aware of the talents and potential of each employee, stay wise to their hidden talents and perspectives.

Awareness is also a continuous state of becoming informed. Leaders are wise to hone their listening for many reasons, one of the most important being detecting untapped potential. Becoming informed is a process whereby leaders listen carefully for words and actions, logic and emotions, and victories and failures. Starbucks showed their willingness to listen and therefore understood the frustration of their minority customers. That awareness led to change that benefited the strategic operation.

It took me a while, but I try to put deliberate effort into becoming aware of biases and limitations of thoughts I may have about myself and people around me. I do not think I was wrong in action when I failed to engage my sister in the evening play time. It's just that I did not know any different than what my bias told me.

----

[47] dictionary.com

I have travelled and worked at several places outside of North America. It is so interesting to observe cultural biases. When I am in a restaurant in some of the countries in South Asia and when I am dining out with my family there is no question that the server will hand me the bill by default, even if it is dinner my wife is buying. If I am the only adult middle-aged male in the group, I must be the breadwinner and, hence, the decision-maker and host of the dinner. That is the pattern the server has likely seen in their family and that is what they experiences close to hundred percent of their time at work. Thus the bias becomes—and remains—belief.

Being informed is the first step of being knowledgeable. Think of this as the process of gaining knowledge. Knowledge is the working capital a leader gains from listening. Awareness is recognizing the value of that capital for improving the organization. Not every leader recognizes DEI as a precious resource or sees the difference between leading and following. That tremendous potential is a rich, complex reserve in the hands of those of us who are alert to future opportunities and obstacles.

Awareness is sophistication: understanding how, when, and where to best leverage this capital. Without that understanding and wise decision-making, considerable resources will be wasted.

Kodak lacked awareness of the changing technology trends around them and its potential impact on their revenue stream. They chose to be ignorant instead of vigilant in following technology trends— especially those concerning their cash cow, film. At the same time, they ignored or dismissed awareness of organizational disaster by refusing to change. Thus they declined, even when they were one of the early organizations to build a digital camera. They chose to stick their heads in the proverbial sand, setting it aside for fear it would ruin their film and accessories business. You know the rest of the story. Kodak ran out of business.

For the context of this book, awareness of the dimensions of diversity—environmental, organizational, social, and personal—is the first important step.

When we have awareness of the dimensions of diversity, we implicitly start to become aware of the following in ourselves and our teams:

- Hidden opportunities,
- Potential problems,
- Insightful perspectives,
- Untapped energy,
- Unintended consequences,
- Outdated attitudes,
- Skills that could be honed,
- Knowledge that hasn't been leveraged,
- Goals that are too small or misguided.

ACCEPTANCE

The second piece to implementing DEI is Acceptance. Awareness is great, but without acknowledging and affirming that each individual has something valuable to offer, there is no trajectory for a better future. To accept DEI means to receive, affirm, be accountable, and state publicly. While this may sound very similar to awareness, acceptance implies actively, rather than passively, working based on what you know and have seen.

- To receive information is to actively recognize what you have and what that knowledge can do for your organization and for the individual. Notice how receiving is not passive. It is purposeful.
- The next step of accepting is affirming both the receipt of the knowledge and the value of the knowledge. Again, affirmation cannot be seen as passive. That means that you, the leader, must take the necessary action or be seen as unaware.
- Any acceptance implies accountability. Once a leader has received information, whether good or bad, potentially harmful

or helpful, they are responsible. They must act. They cannot claim, "I did not know."

- That acceptance as a leader also includes publicly affirming responsibility. Since a leader's role always includes communicating with various individuals and groups, accepting the awareness involves actively communicating with the appropriate people.

As one of my very thoughtful colleagues would say, "A leader needs to do things loudly." Being loud helps with setting and reinforcing the example. For clarity, *loud* in this context means *visibly, assertively, responsibly*. It does not mean *aggressive* or *pushy*.

BELIEF

When awareness and acceptance are in place to a high degree, we act based on that which ultimately turns into belief. Merriam-Webster defines the verb *believe* as "to consider to be true and to hold as an opinion." To believe is to actively choose what one will become aware of and to what level one accepts it. Notice it is not passively following what everyone else is saying or doing. To accept is to actively take responsibility.

Believing in DEI is actively taking a stand in your mind and in the workplace and life. It understands the principles you stand on and the degree to which you believe them. Belief is the opposite of hypocrisy, saying one thing and doing another. Instead, to move the needle with DEI requires standing on our beliefs that DEI is not only the right thing to do, treating everyone equitably, but also that DEI has a high ROI that will greatly benefit the organization, people, and ultimately society.

Kodak believed their future was in their past success. They refused to believe the world was changing. They became aware only as the world left them behind. In the same way, many hold to their prejudice and belief that staying course with similar-looking and -minded people is the easiest strategy and action. But we are wise to ask why we are prejudiced and where these beliefs came from.

Many are not aware of where our prejudice comes from or the level to which they operate under its influence. But when we dig deeper, many of us find our beliefs are based on opinions, not facts, from our existing limited perspective, and we become unaccepting because of this limited perspective. Operating within monocultural worlds means one example is all that is needed to vilify an ethnicity that is rarely encountered. Even in diverse communities, it can be simpler to hang on to one's beliefs than understand the world from another person's perspective. In many ways, it is easier to believe the simple, prejudiced assessment than continually work on updating our beliefs based on the individual we come across or the experience we encounter.

Notice how those prejudicial beliefs arise often out of a lack of awareness.

Broken Patterns

There is a theory that illuminates our arrogant perspective. Yale researchers Anton Gollwitzer and John Bargh argue that a lack of awareness and unaccepting of DEI comes down to *broken patterns*. These researchers contend that as humans, we like life—especially our social world—neatly organized into clean patterns that reduce life's uncertainty. We don't feel safe when our patterns are broken.

Our safe patterns are broken when someone new enters who doesn't look or act like us. We develop prejudice toward anyone or anything that is different because it triggers fear. Their beliefs, values, and actions offend us simply because they are different. With that pattern disrupted, we feel threatened and quickly deem them "inferior" or "less than" because they don't fit the pattern. The logical action, according to this theory, is to exclude them.[48]

This theory of broken patterns seems to make the most sense as the in-group majority will do whatever is necessary to maintain their power. Arrogantly maintaining what they believe are clean,

---

[48] Gollwitzer and Bargh, 2018.

established patterns, such as tradition and history, ensures that those who have been in power will stay in power. We feel safest when we are the insiders enjoying privilege.

These safe patterns of exclusion are present in any culture regardless of race, gender, country, or class. People of color reject those that are "too dark" or "not dark enough." The "no snitch" practice maintains the dominant culture and rejects the police or other outside intervention. Religious institutions hold true to their beliefs and have policies about those breaking from them. Some religious institutions practice excommunication, while corporations decline to hire or terminate employees in their attempts to include or exclude. Politicians create laws separating the included from the excluded. The ultimate intolerance of broken patterns finds dictators like Adolph Hitler strategically murdering dissenters. Each of these organizations would defend its practices to claim the value of that established pattern. Many are unaware that they are non-inclusive. They are also unaware of the negative consequences of their beliefs.

It starts when we are children. The "popular kids' do not include the unpopular ones in their activities. From those early days, we separate into groups and create a hierarchy of good and bad, smart or stupid, potentially successful or failure-bound. Inclusion and exclusion begin early and become second nature through these ingrained patterns we imagine are safe.

Forcing inclusion often creates animosity as those in power do not give up their exclusive power comfortably. This is especially true when some sincerely believe those excluded are not physically, intellectually, emotionally, or spiritually worthy. The slave owner did not see the African as equal and went to war to protect his right to that belief. Even after the North prevailed and slavery was abolished, the majority refused to include the person of color economically, socially, or legally. To this day, most places of worship are informally segregated. Despite being legally allowed, races or people of different faith rarely intermingle in worship services. Notice what that says about broken patterns and arrogant beliefs. Notice how the lack of awareness and acceptance creates exclusion.

In the same way, many men of the 19th century in the U.S. believed women were not equal intellectually. These men fought a legal and social war but ultimately lost. Some still resist including women as equals in politics, business, or entertainment. They cling to their dated beliefs that women don't belong, in order to protect their "Good Old Boys" network.

LGBTQ+ people have fought a similar war to gain inclusion. In each of these cases, the included vehemently rejected the excluded. They arrogantly clung to their beliefs that claimed their small, exclusive group was superior. However, public awareness has changed, and acceptance has greatly increased, leading to many laws changing.

Other times, changing beliefs requires first changing laws and government policies, which requires intense and prolonged activism. Remember, those in power will not relinquish their power easily. Those arrogant, exclusionary beliefs are institutionalized in biased practices that ensure the ruling class remains in power, such as redlining.

Redlining was a practice used by banks to restrict bank funding mortgages. Red lines were drawn on maps, outlining sections of a city deemed "bad risks" for loans. Notice it wasn't based on the individual's ability to repay but on where they lived. Anyone living within those redlined communities couldn't get a bank loan to start a business and improve their lot in life or the community.

Despite being outlawed fifty years ago, the practice negatively impacts those communities today in some ways:

> *Access to credits—home mortgage and small business loans— is an underpinning of economic inclusion and wealth-building in the U.S. Credit access, however, varies greatly depending on individual creditworthiness and also on place-based factors like economic conditions of prosperity and growth, which shape local credit markets… Redlining—the practice of denying borrowers access to credit based on the location of properties*

in minority or economically disadvantaged neighborhoods—was widely practiced across the U.S., While overt redlining is illegal today, having been prohibited under the Fair Housing Act of 1968, its enduring effect is still evident in the structure of U.S. cities.[49]

Notice how establishing laws shapes exclusion and biases the playing field at the time and even long after the laws have been repealed. Arrogant beliefs become stubborn practices that are difficult to change and create a lasting legacy. Exclusionary beliefs become engrained in the psyche of the included and the excluded. Those living outside the redlined areas see a different world with many great opportunities, while those inside the redlined areas struggle to see any opportunities. Those beliefs become stubborn, the foundation upon which the excluded and the included build their lives.

Awareness – acceptance – belief is a progression that benefits leaders and businesses around the globe. In a world of continual and significant change, we are wise to reconsider our awareness level, what we accept, and how arrogantly we are clinging to outdated beliefs. At the same time, we will find growth opportunities when we intentionally become aware of what we currently do not know. By accepting what we find, instead of dismissing it, we build beliefs that become the raw materials for tomorrow's success.

Beyond KPI Metrics

My experience leading teams and interacting with various global stakeholders helped me understand the need for this progression. Awareness and acceptance are overlooked steps, rarely discussed in managerial or executive meetings. We often talk about unconscious bias, but do not speak enough of how to systemically address the same. Increasing awareness and acceptance is that answer.

---

[49] ncrc.org

I am especially conscious of the recent emphasis on inclusion in organizations today. Many, if not most, corporations are hiring large consulting firms to help organizations assess their current state of DEI. As I have watched, read, and researched, I have become aware of a trend. Identifying a handful of KPIs is often seen as the answer. Consultants are hired and measure metrics, providing a number that becomes a statistic and sometimes a standard.

I am concerned that sometimes this approach is too narrow and superficial. The impact is not in the hearts and minds of people. As a result sustainable changes are not happening.

DEI needs to expand beyond a limited list of KPIs that is limited to a predetermined set of questions. It is acceptable to start measuring a few metrics and move out with concentric circles. However, the *viewpoint* or *intent* needs to be bigger than the metrics. That restricted view will never reveal the true picture of an organization's inclusiveness. One must work beyond quick surveys and checklists to become aware of and accept what each employee and the mix of very different employees can offer the organization. Unfortunately, I have often seen organizations treat DEI in a compliance approach instead of as a resource that is valuable.

That is not to say that KPIs are not or cannot be valuable. KPIs serve a valuable function, especially as an entry point into the world of DEI. Leaders should establish a baseline and then begin with a few KPI-driven changes. For many, especially those reluctant to embrace DEI, simply establishing a baseline may seem like significant progress.

Changing this belief system that DEI is a valuable business and social capital rather than a compliance matter is a journey that needs to be taken, and it needs to begin at the very top. As with any other aspect of corporate culture, it will not be successful unless executives lead the change. Only then will it be embraced and cascade to the managers and front-line employees. Without the executives who are fully aware of the potential and who accept both the challenge and the urgency, DEI becomes another fading compliance project. To ensure sustained success, executives must be aware, accepting, and believe in DEI.

A commitment to DEI also cannot be passive or inauthentic. This will not work. Instead, there must be a *genuine* awareness, acceptance, and belief shift from the board through the executives, leader and to the frontline. Yet another formal presentation using PowerPoint will not cut it. Establishing equity as a foundational principle is more caught than taught. Employees at large will believe it once they see the organization consistently and fairly using it. Therefore, starting with themselves leaders must change the awareness and acceptance of the current workforce and move strategically toward becoming the future, inclusive workforce.

The shift starts with awareness. What we do not know, we cannot appreciate. What we do not know, we cannot accept. What we do not know makes us blind to our potential. Without awareness, acceptance, and changing our beliefs, we are destined to be destroyed by what we did not anticipate.

2X2 MODEL

Both Peter Drucker and W. Edward Deming are credited with the notion that you cannot improve or manage what you don't measure. If it is not measured, one is never confident that they are working on the right problem or achieving the desired success. The challenge in our discussion is, "How do we measure our organizational awareness, acceptance, and beliefs if a handful of metrics are not enough?"

To that end, I have created a 2x2 model that we will discuss below and an accompanying assessment approach to be detailed in the remaining chapters. I envision awareness and acceptance working on the X and Y axes and forming a framework, where exclusion reflects the lowest levels of awareness and acceptance and inclusion reflects highest levels of awareness and acceptance.

Ultimately, this diagram and subsequent assessment tool reveal how to measure an organization's inclusivity score.

2x2 Model

Awareness and Acceptance 2x2 model

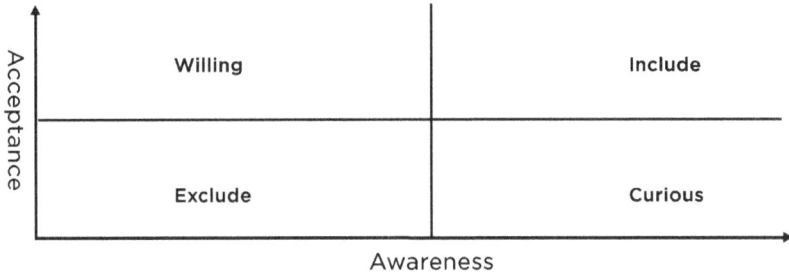

	Willing		Include
Acceptance	Exclude		Curious

Awareness

Exclude

Beginning with the lowest ratings for both Awareness and Acceptance, we find exclusion. Exclusion occupies the lower left quadrant. Those who rate here are failing to be aware of the dimensions of diversity and the value of accepting them in life and work.

Curious

Those rating high on awareness but low on acceptance have enough knowledge to be curious but are not taking the necessary action. It is good to be aware, but without the action associated with acceptance, this becomes a car with a powerful engine and no drivetrain.

When organizations, through various learnings and nudges, get to the point where they are receptive to more information, facts, and data, they are open from the thinking perspective. They are open to trying, for example, delivering from different geographies or delivering certain functions from low-cost centers. From this perspective, the organization is curious about the potential in becoming inclusive. There has been enough excitement; enough data points fit into the organization and the organization has observed it to know they are curious.

When the organization is curious as a result of its awareness of different aspects and dimensions of diversity together at a high level, they are usually ready to make more progress. It will then become important to reinforce the nudges and inputs to keep the organization at the high level of awareness which keeps their readiness and curiosity score high and sets the stage for willing exploration. Like most things in life, this is a dynamic state. A curious organization requires regular care and feeding to stay at that level because the context is always evolving.

Willing

The opposite is also true. Those rating high in acceptance but rating low in awareness are willing, which is also encouraging. Willingness is extremely valuable, as is curiosity, but without awareness of knowledge, willingness is a lot of energy and interest which requires direction. In that sense, being curious about something and failing to act is a waste of valuable time and resources. If you are willing enough to accept potential, do your due diligence and become aware of the situation.

A willing organization often has some portion of the leadership who are open to and believe that there might be value in accepting diversity. But they are not yet aware of the value in diversity's breadth of dimensions. Their awareness and understanding is not at a point to apply their willingness into action with accountability.

Include

The ultimate top right quadrant on this 2x2 diagram is to rate high on awareness and acceptance. This leads to inclusion because an organization or individual that rates in this quadrant is both willing and curious.

The 2x2 diagram demonstrates how to think about the entire journey to diversity as a framework for where an organization stands at the current state and what action plan it can create to move towards inclusivity.

CONCLUSION

To move the needle within our businesses, we need to become aware of the diversity dimensions and appreciate their value. This also includes knowing the shortcomings and opportunities that DEI brings us which help leaders accept challenges and change their antiquated beliefs. Once an organization can measure its progress, opportunities will emerge. However, without awareness and acceptance, we are destined to be stuck with our existing beliefs.

KEY TAKEAWAYS

- Awareness is the starting point for significant change.
- Sustained action, when augmented with awareness, leads to acceptance.
- Progression in awareness and acceptance leads to an upgrade of our belief system, which makes us relevant and valuable.

CHAPTER 8:

ASSESSMENT

It is important to assess our current state and to continually assess our progress in the journey from exclusion to inclusion. Individuals, organizations, and departments can all effectively use the framework I described in the previous chapter to do so.

An organization's position in the framework of Awareness Acceptance (2x2) could be considered the aggregation of its stakeholders' awareness and acceptance score. For our purposes here, stakeholders include the workforce, management, c-suite, and any others who are impacted by or directly impact the organization's services and products.

The key objective of assessment is to arrive at actionable insights. However, traditional assessment models do not always provide these results because typical surveys provide results that do not actually indicate the true state of the organization. For example, it is not unusual for traditional surveys to result in higher scores for DEI metrics. When asked about sensitive topics like DEI, survey respondents often choose the "right" answer instead of the true statement unless they apply enough thoughtfulness.

As I stated in one of my previous books, *Leadership 4.0*, "Technology is commodity and People are the differentiators." The same belief applies in this space. Successfully assessing any organization with 2x2 must start with individual assessments performed by each internal or external stakeholder. Once individual assessments have been made, scores can be aggregated for a stakeholder set (which can include the entire organization, a department, or any other combination of stakeholders).

As organizations traverse to their journey towards the target top right quadrant, the first step is to assess and plot our organization on this 2x2 matrix. We will explore this step a bit more in this chapter as we discuss the best approach for conducting the assessment at an individual level and then consider assessments at the organizational level (and how to plot results in the 2x2 grid).

In the following chapter, we will talk about potential action we can take along our journey to inclusion.

WHY ASSESSMENT?

Let's first talk about the need for assessment. When we go to a personal care professional, say a dietician or a personal trainer, the first thing they typically do is assess your current state. From there, they usually try to understand your goals so they can then create an action plan to achieve the same.

The 2x2 framework performs a parallel function. It is the tool which will help assess current and future states while also helping track progress in a structured and sustainable manner.

The 2x2 method is more effective than traditional surveys because it avoids the pitfalls that create inauthentic results. I would have liked to include a prescriptive survey in this book, to make it even easier for readers to use the 2x2 for personal and eventually organizational assessment. But there is a catch. As I have already pointed out, most traditional surveys ask about opinions on diversity. Regardless of personal awareness and acceptance level, responders are aware of the "right" answer to questions for typical surveys in case of DEI.

Responders are often careful, and their bias skews towards answers in favor of those answers when asked through traditional survey questions. Individual attempts to answer "correctly" on a traditional survey often misguide organizations.

Before I introduce my recommendations to measure awareness and acceptance, let me give an example of a standard, often-used DEI questionnaire which typically measures opinion instead of true awareness:

> Please rate your agreement with the following statements on a scale of 1 to 5, where 5 strongly agree, and 1 is not at all agree.
>
> • When interacting with people with limited English language skills, I always keep in mind that limited English language skills don't reflect their intelligence or literacy level in their preferred language.

More than 80 percent of respondents will answer 4 or 5 to the first option, but this does not reflect their awareness or acceptance. So we must ask ourselves what good these results provide and what needs to happen differently.

First and foremost, to answer accurately and honestly, responders must feel safe and comfortable in their environment—and these types of questions, phrased in this way, do not create that safety and comfort. We have to understand and acknowledge that these are hard questions for any respondent, and that we all struggle with the broken patterns discussed in the previous chapter.

It is helpful to remember that awareness is not about measuring an individual's opinion about diversity. Rather, it is a measure of how much knowledge they have about the breadth of diversity's dimensions. In other words, this measure is a *knowledge check*, not a typical survey. Testing someone's knowledge of diversity dimensions should be interesting and fact-based.

The facts around diversity dimensions change with factors like location, time, and other everyday circumstances. Leveraging current and relevant facts to assess awareness measures is important to creating a dynamic knowledge check that will be a useful part of a training program in any organization.

Measuring Awareness in the 2x2 Grid

To achieve this goal, the awareness assessment should take the form of a trivia-style questionnaire. It should include DEI facts that are relevant to the context of the organization, and it should be treated like any other knowledge area in which the organization's learning and development team might be engaged. The trivia could also have multiple levels as the organization progresses through the journey and improves the awareness quotient through deliberate action and training.

Below is an example of an awareness assessment trivia for a North American tech organization. Other organizations can use this example as a template for their own assessment, but should update its questions based on changing statistics, time, and context.

Example of an Awareness Assessment for Kelstra, a North American Tech Company

Each reader is encouraged to take the DEI trivia quiz and check their own score. Answers are included after the questionnaire. This trivia does not ask for opinions. Rather, is focused on metrics and facts meant to gauge general awareness of DEI. When tested with several well-read professionals, more than 50 percent scored less than 50 percent.

AWARENESS TRIVIA EXAMPLE

To celebrate culture and diversity here at (insert organization name), we've gathered some trivia questions to assess your awareness of diversity dimensions. Having a deep awareness of diversity dimensions opens up new ways of thinking and helps us be more intentional around people from various backgrounds, races, and cultures. We hope you enjoy answering these 10 fun, fact-based questions. When you are finished, go ahead and calculate your awareness score using the marking key. Be true to yourself—don't use Google! Answer the questions based on your awareness.

QUESTIONS

1. As of October 2021, what proportion of Millennials in the US are non-white?
   - Less than 5 percent
   - 18 percent
   - 24 percent
   - 43 percent

2. 57 percent of people in state prisons for drug offenses in the US are African American. What percentage of illicit drug users in the overall US population are African American?
   - 14 percent
   - 28 percent
   - 42 percent
   - 56 percent

3. In a study conducted by the National Bureau of Economic Research, researchers replied to help-wanted ads by sending résumés from fictitious applicants. How much more likely were applicants with stereotypically White names to get a callback regarding their applications than applicants with stereotypically Black names?
   - 15 percent more likely
   - 26 percent more likely
   - 39 percent more likely
   - 50 percent more likely

4. Do all transgender people have gender-confirming surgery?
   - Yes
   - No

5. In the US, if the current trend continues, by which year will the number of Muslims nearly equal the number of Christians?
   - 2030
   - 2050
   - 2060
   - 2070

6. In what proportion of US households are mothers the sole breadwinners?
   - 15 percent
   - 22 percent
   - 35 percent
   - 47 percent

7. What does BIPOC stand for?
   - Black, Indigenous, and People of Color
   - Bisexual, Intersectional People of Color
   - Black, Intersectional Persons of Culture
   - Bisexual, Indigenous People of Color

8. A heterosexual woman participates in a Pride Parade and actively advocates for LGBTQ+ rights in the workplace. This woman is a(n) .... to the LGBTQ+ community.
   - Ally
   - BIPOC
   - Albinism
   - Activist

9. A University is under scrutiny for a lack of diversity on campus. The University does not change any of its admission policies or resources but begins using photos of Black students in its

marketing materials to give a superficial appearance of equality. This is an example of:

- Tokenism

- Critical Race Theory

- Classism

- Intersectionality

10. Xenophobia is:
    - A system of oppression based on the fear, hatred, or mistrust of that which is foreign, especially strangers or people from different countries or cultures.

    - When someone from a non-marginalized group professes to support and solidarity with a marginalized group in a way that either isn't helpful or actively harms that group.

    - A system of oppression that works against the young and the old and values individuals of a particular age range.

    - Refers specifically to how institutional policies and practices create different outcomes for different racial groups.

It is recommended to keep the trivia to less than 30 questions so the employee can finish within less than 30 mins. Remember, measuring *knowledge*—not *opinion*—is key to this part of awareness assessment.

AWARENESS TRIVIA ANSWER KEY

1. 43 percent
2. 14 percent
3. 50 percent more likely
4. No
5. 2050
6. 47 percent
7. Black, Indigenous, and people of color
8. Ally
9. Tokenism
10. A system of oppression based on the fear, hatred, or mistrust of that which is foreign, especially strangers or people from different countries or cultures.

SCORING THE AWARENESS TRIVIA FOR INDIVIDUALS

Each awareness question in the trivia is worth 1 point. If an individual got all ten questions correct, then the total score will add up to 10. To fit this score in the 2x2 grid where the axis is 5 units, we have to normalize the score. The normalized score for an individual will be (total score/n), where n is the normalizing factor that fits the score into the grid scale. In this case, since there are 10 questions, the normalizing factor is $n=10/5=2$. If there were 20 questions, $n=20/5=4$. If the number of questions is 30, n will be 6. And so on.

Calculating the normalized score in the trivia example in the previous page for an individual who got all questions correct looks like this:

Normalized score = 10/2, which is 5.

If someone had 5 correct answers, their score would be 5/normalized factor(n); n being 2 in the example provided. The score plotted in the 2x2 grid for this individual will be (5/2)=2.5. If someone got 8 questions correct in the 10 question awareness trivia, the score to be plotted in the grid will be (8/2)=4.

I will talk about how to aggregate individual-level scores to organizational awareness score calculations later in this chapter.

ACCEPTANCE

As we discussed in the 2x2 grid in the previous chapter, awareness expands our perspective and generates willingness. However, awareness alone fails to move the needle.

Instead, awareness must lead to appropriate action by which individuals of all demographics are welcomed and valued. Acceptance is found in the organization's action to create inclusive policies, mission and vision statements, and everyday practices. While awareness is grounded in knowledge and understanding, acceptance is the window into the organization's behavior. Acceptance shows the state of mind from which the organization creates or denies daily opportunities. In the end, action proves that an organization exists on the spectrum of inclusion and exclusion.

Acceptance is the state of mind necessary to accept diversity in an actionable, daily manner. A quick and easy way to measure acceptance is to review an organization's demographics. What percentage of your workforce is a minority? Is that percentage below 50? If so, it is difficult to claim you are inclusive. An organization should also ask what percentage of its executives are minorities and what percentage of its supervisors and managers are minorities. Without diversity at those levels, and organization cannot be considered inclusive.

The following are seven useful dimensions of acceptance:

1. **Fair treatment:** Employees at my organization who help the organization achieve its strategic objectives are rewarded and recognized fairly.

2. **Integrating differences:** Employees at my organization respect and value each other's opinions.

3. **Decision making:** Members of my team fairly consider ideas and suggestions offered by other team members.

4. **Psychological safety:** I feel welcome to express my true feelings at work.

5. **Trust:** The communication we receive from the organization is honest and open.

6. **Belonging:** People in my organization care about me.

7. **Diversity:** Managers at my organization are as diverse as the broader workforce.

While these seven categories are valuable, I have found that traditional surveys are limited in their results because of their tendency to measure opinion instead of any employee's true state of mind. Again, the problem stems from the fact that respondents want to say what is right, and therefore create a type of test bias that is more telling about their motivations than about their knowledge and beliefs concerning diversity. When we respond to any kind of survey, we may simply want to fit in, so we answer with what we believe is the politically appropriate (correct) answer. We may also hide our true feelings or beliefs to protect ourselves from negative consequences. Finally, we want to feel better about ourselves, so we inflate our answers and self-esteem.

This inflated test bias may be especially compelling when measuring DEI. Answering honestly may mean going against popular opinion and company policy. Fearing isolation, career stagnation, or even termination, respondents keep their heads down and parrot the correct answers. When that happens, the survey results are meaningless.

Instead, the best acceptance metric is accomplished by measuring the opportunities an organization makes available. If the organization is truly inclusive, it offers opportunities because they believe each is valuable and are curious about what each can offer to improve the organization. However, if the organization chooses not to make these opportunities available, no matter what they say, they are not accepting.

Measuring Acceptance

Moving beyond simple survey questions to more behavioral and storytelling techniques will help gauge acceptance. Thus there are two possible ways to assess the acceptance score for the 2x2 grid.

1. Psychometric assessment
2. Case study (behavioral interview) based assessment

Advanced psychometric questions like those posed in a Birkman Assessment ask for and contain the history and collective knowledge from millions of assessments over years. These highly honed surveys use questions that have been tweaked over many years in an effort to prevent biases and adjustments. While these are valuable, most leaders don't have the time, energy, expertise, or resources to create a unique assessment. And the options are limited when it comes to such a model. This is especially true for DEI as it is a relatively new topic.

Instead, utilize a storytelling rubric that allows employees to tell their story honestly, and use it understand their perspective better. Then you can use these stories to assess the acceptance score for individuals and the organization as a whole.

Before I get into the details of this story-based acceptance scoring method, I would like to say that I understand that a purely quantitative traditional survey will be much easier to implement. That said, the contextual and the qualitative aspects of the topic are equally important. As a result, a story telling approach to assessment that is admittedly more complex is worth the effort because it will provide much higher value input from the assessment perspective.

An additional advantage of this approach is that since the individual taking the assessment is scoring someone else's story, there is no added pressure to providing the 'right' or acceptable answers.

Here is an example of how it would work.

To run the assessments long term, organizations need to have wide variety or real-life stories collected over time to form a "story bank." To maintain enough stories in the story bank, capture and inventory them through ERG (Employee Resource groups) and other individual and group interactions.

First, invite a set of individuals who are willing and interested to tell their story. You can ask them to submit the story anonymously or encourage story telling as part of ERG discussions, but keep in mind that the assessment will be far more valuable when they feel safe enough to put their name on it. Ask the individual to tell *their* story, reminding them that any story has a beginning, middle, and end (which brings us to the current moment). Along the way, there are smaller stories of joy or frustration.

Give the individuals who are submitting the story the following guideline:

Please tell me your story of working at (the name of your organization).

Please provide details and examples.

1. When did you start?
2. Why did you choose to work here?
3. How has your career developed?
4. What have you enjoyed or appreciated most?
5. What has frustrated you?

In the storytelling process, also ask them to include the following questions in their answer.

6. **(Fairness)** How have you been fairly rewarded and recognized?
7. **(Differences)** Does your team respect and value each other's opinions, despite individual differences?
8. **(Decision Making)** Are decisions based on the merit of the idea or personal bias?
9. **(Psychological Safety)** How safe do you feel expressing your true feelings at work?
10. **(Trust)** How much do you trust your team/leader? Who can you trust within the organization? Why?
11. **(Belonging)** Do you sense that I belong in this organization? This department?
12. **(Diversity)** How much do you identify with the organization?

Once the story bank is built (can range from 5 or 10 stories to as many as you collect), use the stories to assess the acceptance score of individuals and the organization. Collecting stories and refreshing the story bank should be an ongoing activity organization should pursue.

Send a group of stories (about 5 or 10) to employees and stakeholders along with an awareness knowledge check. Ask them to read the stories. Then ask them to rate the dimensions of acceptance from three categories based on the story content. The three categories are: a) very much, b) somewhat, or c) not at all.

EXAMPLE:
STORYTELLING ACCEPTANCE ASSESSMENT

Please read the following stories that have been shared by your fellow coworkers. Next, please rate the stories for the 7 dimensions of acceptance using three categories: a) very much, b) somewhat, or c) not at all.

1. **(Fairness)** Is the individual fairly rewarded and recognized?

2. **(Differences)** Does the team respect and value each other's opinions, despite individual differences?

3. **(Decision Making)** Are decisions based on the merit of the idea or personal bias?

4. **(Psychological Safety)** How safe do you think the individual feels expressing true feelings at work?

5. **(Trust)** How much do you feel the individual trusts the organization/team/leader?

6. **(Belonging)** Do you sense that the individual belong in this organization? This department?

7. **(Diversity**) How much does the individual identify with the organization?

EXAMPLE STORY 1

"I started work at this company six years ago because I needed a job. I didn't know exactly what I wanted to do, so when they offered me a job in the shipping and receiving department, I took it. In the beginning, I didn't even know what they did or what was involved. I just knew the pay was decent and they gave me an opportunity. I enjoyed that my supervisor gave me an opportunity to learn all the aspects of the department. He was fair and rewarded my willingness to learn, even though others had more experience (but were only interested in the paycheck). That paid off two years later when I was promoted to team lead and then, two years after that, promoted to supervisor when the position opened up. I like working for a company that continually gives me opportunities to learn and grow.

To answer the questions, I very much feel as if I have been rewarded fairly **(Fairness)**. Even when I have wanted a specific job or opportunity and didn't receive it, it was only because someone else was more qualified or needed a chance to show what they could do.

(Differences). I very much like that everybody's opinion matters. Even those people who are only there for the paycheck are valued for the work they provide.

(Decision Making) It can be frustrating that managers seem to be heard more than supervisors. I'm unsure if that is because they are more accomplished or that supervisor are seen as less. I somewhat believe in their decision-making.

(Psychological Safety) For that reason, sometimes, I hold back on offering my opinion. I guess I'm somewhat reserved with my opinion.

(Trust) I have five people that I completely trust. That may be why I believe in this company. My old supervisor is now a manager and always welcomes my input, whether he agrees or not. I also trust three other managers and the CEO. They all take the time to listen and provide honest feedback. Of course, a few people always have a personal agenda, but I stay clear of them. I rate the trust as very much even though I don't trust everyone.

(Belonging). I sense that I very much belong at this company because of the trust.

(Diversity). When I was first hired, I didn't see many people who looked like me. That was rather frustrating. But now I see a very diverse mix and that is very encouraging. I'm very much impressed."

EXAMPLE STORY 2

"I started work at this company 8 years ago because I needed a job. I didn't know exactly what I wanted to do so when they offered me a job in the shipping and receiving department, I took it. From the beginning, I didn't even know what they did or what was involved. All I knew was that the pay was decent, and they gave me the job.

It's been pretty frustrating because they seem to play favorites. Certain people get good jobs, while others of us never really get the opportunity. Their opinion matters but not mine or any of my friends. For example, the supervisor has two of his favorites that get good jobs. No wonder they are being considered for promotion. Meanwhile, others are told we don't have the experience. I've been here eight years and hate coming to work. The only thing keeping me is the money.

To answer the questions, I very much feel as if I have not been rewarded fairly **(Fairness)**. I can learn as well as any of those others, but I never get the opportunity.

(Differences). My opinion doesn't matter, nor do any of my friends' opinions.

(Decision Making) You got to be one of them to matter. Despite what they claim in their diversity training and departments, you must look and think like them to get anywhere in this company. One of these pet employees said they would never listen to me unless I started working harder. They only want to hear what they already know. I'd quit, but I can't find a job that pays as well as this one.

(Psychological Safety) My opinion doesn't matter. If I stated my mind, I'd be fired. Go to work, shut up, do what's required and move on. That's all they get.

(Trust) The only ones I trust are my friends. Nobody in management cares.

(Belonging). I don't belong here but I don't know where else I belong.

(Diversity). No, they hire and promote their own. The rest of us just don't cut it in their eyes."

ACCEPTANCE SCORES AT AN INDIVIDUAL LEVEL BASED ON THE 7 DIMENSIONS OF ACCEPTANCE

(Scoring Example Story 1 by an individual taking the assessment.)

Fairness...Very Much – 3 points

Differences...Very Much – 3 points

Decision Making ....Somewhat – 2 points

Psychological Safety...Somewhat - 2 points

Trust..Very Much - 3 points

Belonging ....Very Much - 3 points

Diversity...Very Much -3 Points

Total.. **19/21**

(Scoring Example Story 2 by an individual taking the assessment)

Fairness...Very Little – 1 point

Differences...Very Little – 1 point

Decision Making ....Very Little – 1 point

Psychological Safety...Very Little - 1 point

Trust..Very Little - 1 point

Belonging ....Very Little - 1 point

Diversity..Very Little - 1 point

Total...**7/21**

Assume there are 10 such stories which are used in each individual assessment. As in the case of awareness, to fit into the 2x2 awareness and acceptance grid, we scale the total story score by a normalization factor (the total number of stories divided by 5; 5 being the grid scale). So, if there are 10 stories included in an individual assessment, the normalization scale factor would be $n = 10/5 = 2$

The net acceptance score at an individual level will be the sum of each story score divided by the normalization scale factor:

$$(x1+ x2 + ... +x10)/n.$$

PLOTTING THE AWARENESS/ACCEPTANCE GRID AT THE INDIVIDUAL LEVEL

Net acceptance score is then plotted on the grid, with awareness score on the X-Axis and acceptance score on the Y-Axis.

PLOTTING THE AWARENESS/ACCEPTANCE GRID AT THE ORGANIZATION LEVEL

For an organization or department, the awareness score will be the sum of individual awareness scores divided by the total number of stakeholders taking the awareness assessment. Similarly, the department or organization's acceptance score will be sum of individual acceptance scores divided by number of stakeholders taking the acceptance assessment.

Let's assume for Kelstra, the tech company used in this example, that the awareness score was 2 and the acceptance score was 1.5. When plotted on the 2x2 framework, it will be plotted as below:

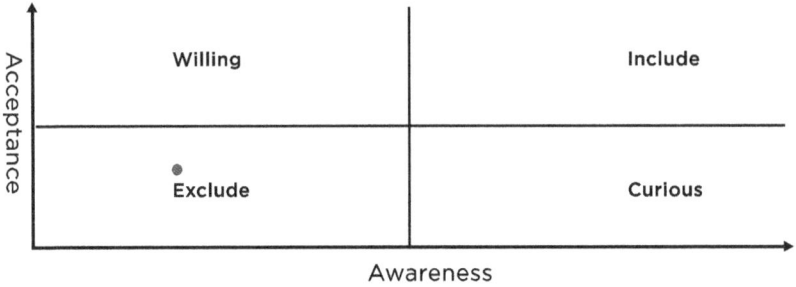

How and When to Assess

Another important aspect of assessment is knowing the right way and time to perform it. It is absolutely critical that assessment is built in a dynamic way, so that questions and levels are modified based on the organization's journey and state of maturity. Also, the level or variety of questions is important from an engagement perspective.

Organizations could launch a program around DEI, provide context to stakeholders, and launch this assessment for a baseline. But on an ongoing basis, it is important to bake these assessments into various existing training and assessment in other areas of business. For example, most large organizations have an annual process of mandatory training and assessment built around their code of conduct. Often organizations effectively include assessments related to awareness and acceptance just as they would for safety or cyber security.

Assessment, like DEI, should be a strategic element that is connected to every department and embedded within every action plan. It shouldn't be limited to annual reviews but used as an ongoing measurement of a vibrant organization that is continually transforming itself.

I personally like the fact-based trivia around assessment of awareness like the example provided above, as it gives employees a sense of gaining real knowledge and something they often take home and share with their kids or family. The story telling for acceptance is so much more engaging, real, and powerful. I recommend it over opinion surveys.

Participation

Any successful assessment requires good participation. Here are some ways to increase your employees' participation in awareness and acceptance assessments:

- DEI should not be a politically correct club used to beat an employee into obedience, especially through the threat of termination and career consequences. Instead, position these assessments as a valuable source of input from employees in an effort to know them better—and show the organizations' genuine sincerity.

- Design the assessments so they are concise, interesting, and simple to complete. We live in a fast-paced world of reduced attention spans. Notice the awareness questionnaire was only 10 items. Help folks express their awareness and acceptance quickly but accurately.

- Provide a "don't know, no opinion, or not applicable" option where possible. While you don't want to give respondents an easy way to avoid answering a question, be honest in constructing the quiz. Remember, this is a listening tool to gauge where they are in their approach to diversity, equity, and inclusion.

- Eliminate leading questions. Again, this should be a listening experience through which you better understand your employees. Non-inclusive beliefs are likely taught during childhood and reinforced during adulthood. Often those who are non-inclusive have grown up in isolation and fear the broken patterns posed by inclusion. Assessment questions should serve to understand, not change, the beliefs. Also, keep in mind that some exclusive beliefs may have evolved from harmful experiences. Respect where individuals are in their approach. Next, some may have suffered exclusion even though they look like the majority demographic. While not based a demographic quality, they have been judged, deemed inferior, and excluded.

- Lastly, some exclusion is based on pride and fear. My point is that questions must be neutral and honestly assess current acceptance. Remember, there should be no "right" answer.

CONCLUSION

It is hard to improve what we cannot measure. Assessment of our current state with respect to awareness and acceptance is very important—not only to create the baseline for our journey, but also for ongoing assessment of our progress. When performing an assessment, focus on *assessing* and try to avoid getting stuck with opinions. Awareness is really a knowledge check about dimensions of diversity that includes local and relevant facts and data. Acceptance is all about real-life stories that reflect the behavior of the organization in a format which can be scored as discussed above. Successful assessment is measuring the state in the 2x2 framework, which can be tracked and measured through the journey.

KEY TAKEAWAYS:

- Assessment of the current state of awareness and acceptance is one of the most objective yet contextual ways to baseline an organization.

- Assessment needs to be both qualitative and quantitative. Remember, we are talking about a change that involves hearts and minds.

- Stakeholders' comfort and psychological safety is critical for quality and participation in the assessment.

CHAPTER 9:

ACTION

If we continue with the example of the hypothetical tech company used in the previous chapter, the question becomes how the company moves the needle and thrives as it becomes more inclusive.

This chapter will assume that Kelstra, the hypothetical tech company, has low scores in awareness and acceptance as depicted by the 2x2 diagram. They are in the *exclude* quadrant. We can quickly judge Kelstra or work on a path to get them to the *include* quadrant over a period of time and in a structured manner.

Leveraging the 2x2 framework, we will explore actions that take two different paths.

1. Increase awareness by exposing the workforce to knowledge about various diversity dimensions, starting with those which are most relevant for an organization or department. Regularly imparting and reinforcing this knowledge will help the organization move from the exclusion quadrant to curious.

2. Increase acceptance and willingness to act in favor of unlocking the most value through inclusion.

AWARENESS

Let's first examine the action needed to raise awareness and then acceptance.

My breadth of knowledge about diversity was significantly narrow before I started taking an active interest in this topic. Reading, listening, and observing were my vehicles for increasing awareness. I read several books and papers and started connecting the dots in my own way. We are all unique, and our paths to awareness will not all look the same. Nor should they. My path was long and personal. How might an organization achieve required level of knowledge at scale and in a more systemic way?

A challenge of increasing awareness is setting aside our certainty. Awareness and certainty are two sides of the same coin. We cannot become aware until we release our certainty. The ancient philosopher Confucius said, "To know what you know and what you do not know, that is true knowledge." In the same vein, Alvin Toffler said, "The illiterate of the 21st century will not be those who cannot read and write, but those who cannot learn, unlearn, and relearn." We must set aside our certainty to increase our awareness, unlearning what we thought we knew or what worked in the past but no longer works. Increasing awareness is a continual process.

That is especially true with diversity, equity, and inclusion. Our world is constantly changing. As leaders, we must continually sharpen our awareness to avoid becoming antiquated—and to seize the best opportunities.

There is one thing we also know: organizational culture begins at the top. When the CEO and executive team actively drives a change, it will likely happen. If they do not support the change, it likely won't.

If you are a manager or supervisor, you can also contribute and shape your department's culture. Awareness is relevant for all of us. While the level of change you can make in your organization will often depend on the level of your leadership and influence, you still play an active role.

Effective Listening

To move the needle toward awareness of DEI, let's begin with a series of introspective questions. These questions are designed to help us listen more effectively. Too often, leaders are so busy doing and speaking that they ignore taking the time to listen unselfishly to their team. To listen effectively is to set aside your certainty while comprehending what the other person is saying *without judging them*.

That is the core of the problem behind non-inclusive behavior: people don't listen without judging. They assume they know what someone will say and quickly dismiss it as inferior. They exclude because they have already judged. But to listen is to suspend judgment as a way to increase awareness and then gain knowledge. When listening effectively, leaders build relationships by taking the time and energy to understand the situation from the other person's perspective.

Relaxing Our Certainty to Increase Our Potential

We need to relax our certainty because we don't know everything. (Admitting that may be the biggest challenge to increasing awareness.) From there, we must be willing to unlearn what we think we know. We are wise to recognize that the world is changing rapidly and radically. Innovation is evolving; the best practices of yesterday are obsolete today. Like Kodak, we will stagnate and miss the best opportunities if we cling to what we once learned without an awareness of new and improved technology, processes, and perspectives.

Kodak blinded themselves to the potential of the digital camera because they were certain that film was their best product. And for decades, film *was* their best practice—but their certainty that it would continue to be so blinded them. Instead of increasing their awareness by asking the right questions and taking the time and energy to listen, they quickly judged and effectively ran their organization into the ground.

In the same way, non-inclusive leaders ignore the potential of a diverse workforce. Most importantly, they overlook diverse thinking by blinding themselves with their dogmatic beliefs that uniformity and obedience ensure the best productivity and profits. Sadly, that blindness is preventing them from achieving their peak potential. The kind of uniformity they espouse may have worked at one point, but it limits organizations today.

It Starts With You

Increasing awareness of your organization starts with awareness of yourself. Begin by listening more and talking less. Investigate the hidden potential that your organization is overlooking, then consider how it might be affecting the company's bottom line. Detail how the diversity of perspectives and hidden talents you find can benefit the organization. Gather specific examples.

Imagine working in a manufacturing plant and discovering that truckloads of waste material were discarded each day. Then imagine that you discovered how to repurpose that waste to generate more profits and reduce emissions. Would you share that information with the organization? Of course you would.

Now, imagine someone very introverted identified this solution and the person did not feel included. They might not ever bring it up, or they might bring it up too late. Perhaps the person is used to being overlooked because of their lack of seniority within the company, used to having their ideas ignored by its leaders. The result is a damaging one: they keep quiet while a potentially game-changing idea goes undiscovered. This scenario happens every day at work. If we are not aware, ready to park our certainty, and willing to listen to folks regardless of where they belong in the hierarchy, we will miss these important ideas.

From Listening to Speaking

Strategically choose which leaders that will accept your message. Approach them and share your new awareness. Notice that you have moved from listening to purposeful speaking. Within that communication, recognize that you can nudge a person or pass the awareness to them.

Nudging itself can happen in a few ways. Reinforcement of messaging and/or making the messaging visible front and center in the physical or virtual workplaces are common ones. Many activists choose direct, sometimes forceful, communication to convince a listener.

However, *persuasion*—what you are working to accomplish by raising awareness—requires more finesse than brute force. Intrigue and enticement are more likely to convince a listener to willingly change their misguided attitudes into permanent, inclusive beliefs. Meanwhile, forcing your beliefs upon them creates resistance and temporary acceptance that is little more than show. Whenever you share with others, seek to nudge. As the old saying goes, it is easier to attract bees with honey than vinegar. Persuading others with polite requests and a positive attitude rather than with demands and negativity.

Where to Act

Having discussed *how* we share this awareness, let's focus on *where* to share it. Let's get a little more tactical as we examine ways to make your awareness actionable.

Consider increasing awareness through lunch and learn sessions, e-learning, town hall meetings, and small group discussions, in which you can encourage and facilitate one-on-one, private conversations that raise awareness. More creative options include using role play, creating an entertaining video, or staging a play. You can even create an ad campaign to share via digital or hard copy.

For example, take a look at the following ad campaign that was created for International Women's Day 2022 IWD 2022#BREAKTHEBIAS.

Notice the intriguing statements followed by provocative questions in this International Women's Day poster. [50]

2022 IWD compaign

This ad campaign challenges our perceptions by sharing the message in a way that makes us stop and rethink what we are unaware of or have learned to be true.

In the same way, you can move the needle for awareness by asking questions or making statements. You can also raise awareness by telling success stories. This can be accomplished in three

---

[50] https://www.internationalwomensday.com/2022theme, https://cpblondon.com/portfolio/international-womens-day-imagine/

ways: telling the viewer what to believe, inviting them to believe differently, and showing them results meant to influence their beliefs. Each comes with advantages and disadvantages.

The following videos demonstrate these three ways. Each type of video offers nuances for communicating via any medium, including interpersonal and public communication.

First, many diversity videos tell the viewer what to believe. In the first video, for example, *Together, All The Way* by Maersk tells their business story overlayed with a strong message of LGBTQ+ inclusion.[51] In essence, this approach says, "we are different" and "we are valuable." While this is valuable and helps many shift perspectives, individuals with strongly held beliefs about LGBTQ+ may quickly reject it. That said, this type of video may work well to reinforce the beliefs of those who are already inclusive and move them to action.

Another type of diversity video shows people discussing misconceptions in such a way that the viewer is *invited* to believe. In HP's *On Latino Jobs*, the viewer is told about misguided perceptions of Latino workers. We hear these misperceptions spoken by white workers before hearing more accurate views from Latino workers themselves. This video uses the same method as the print campaign above, intriguing the listener to change perspectives.[52] Notice this is a more subtle approach and easier for the exclusive viewer to accept. It also reinforces the beliefs of those who already practice inclusivity.[53]

A third and better way to raise awareness is to *show* viewers the results. Nike's *You Can't Stop Sisters* commercial video doesn't discuss race or gender but shows how two sisters, Venus and Serena Williams, changed the game of tennis.[54] Notice this

---

[51] Maersk - 'Together, All The Way' – An Anthem (©A.P. Moller – Maersk).

[52] Youtube.com. #LatinoJobs | Reinvent Mindsets: Part 4 | HP.

[53] Similarly, Hewlett Packard's *Reinvent Mindset* is also a great example of talking about inclusion by inviting viewers to consider a specific belief.

[54] YouTube.com, Venus & Serena Williams *You Can't Stop Sisters* | Nike Commercial.

video leaves demographics behind and simply focuses on such convincing results that even many otherwise non-inclusive individuals will acknowledge the Williams sisters' success. In that sense, the communication leaps over the problematic question of inclusion and equity. How would it even be possible to exclude them? They are some of the most successful women tennis players in history.

Retest and Stay the Course

Once you have established a flow of information and open communication, periodically retest your organization's awareness. Remember, you seek to increase their knowledge about diversity, the value of a diverse perspective, and how to become more aware and adaptable in a continually changing world.

Also remember that this is a *journey* to knowledge and understanding. Adult education is hard because it requires *un*learning in addition to learning—a process that is definitely harder than simply learning.

Teach, nudge, and test your stakeholders in interesting and engaging ways so that your audience will enjoy learning. Interest and engagement are key to the process, and they come by reaching out and connecting in a diverse manner with stakeholders. No single method of communication will fit every individual. For example, if you give me a printed book or a written recommendation, it is guaranteed I will read it and learn from it. However, my peer—a colleague who is actually more curious and smarter than me—would never read a book, particularly if it is a printed copy. He consumes information in smaller chunks on the internet.

My point is that there is no right or wrong, only different. As we are rolling out and reinforcing awareness, it is critical we do not forget equity in our approach. When we use it as a guiding principle in our efforts, the result will be an organizational shift away from exclusion and toward curiosity.

ACCEPTANCE

Awareness is a fact-based understanding of the degree to which you are conscious of what is happening. It is cognitive and affective, thinking and feeling. Acceptance, however, is behavioral and therefore focused on action. To accept is to pivot your behavior because of something you have become aware of.

In simpler terms, acceptance is *engagement*. At the tactical level, it is a general willingness to take action. In fact, the willingness to engage in diverse thinking often leads to better actions. But until that belief is established, acceptance is still plotted in the *exclude* quadrant and exclusion is still the pattern.

Notice that acceptance takes an active curiosity, not a passive one. Acceptance is a curiosity based upon a willingness to act and include, but the goal must always be inclusive action. Acceptance will not happen if we are unaware and not, therefore, intensely curious about the action.

Acceptance is also about engagement and creating a safe space where the culture allows for open discussions, debates on sensitive topics, and a willingness to learn about what will mobilize each member of the organization towards action. As leaders, you must engage stakeholders on DEI's "why" and "purpose." Acceptance focuses on engagement in the organization, beginning very early in the hiring process. In the case of universities, for example, acceptance engagement begins during interviews and continues through the hiring, onboarding, training, promotion, and on throughout the stakeholder life cycle.

Engagement, Psychological Safety, and Leadership

To improve the score and increase overall acceptance, the focus should be on deliberately engaging in a psychologically safe way.

When engagement and psychological safety in culture work together, acceptance usually increases. Keep in mind, however, that this leg of the journey might take longer. In some cases, it might not happen until an organization sees turnover in its resistant leadership. Hence it is important to work toward establishing and maintaining a leadership pipeline with a higher acceptance score.

I want to very clear on one thing. Adults and their beliefs are not easy to change. There will be organizations and leadership that will go along with the journey simply out of compliance, especially if key leaders within the organization do not actually believe in the need for and value of making the change. Worse, they may be creating a psychologically unsafe environment that works against your attempts to move toward acceptance and inclusion. In such cases, organizations will either have to change the people and/or wait for attrition. I know how harsh that sounds, but it is based on my experience working across geographies and several very large brands.

Remember, "acceptance is action" occurs when your organization is curious about what each individual offers, and that curiosity translates into action, people will start to notice that significant changes are happening.

As I have said, acceptance is harder because it requires individuals to first process the knowledge they gain through improved awareness, then park their certainties and be flexible enough to shift their preexisting beliefs aside to act in a more inclusive manner. In my observation, success comes when leadership lead by example and pivot an organization from "exclude" to "willing."

When awareness and acceptance both tend to improve, an organization travels towards the *Include* quadrant of the 2x2 framework.

Traversing the 2x2 framework as mentioned above is not an insignificant change. It is important for professionals and organizations to understand that the shift is transformational and will require some deliberate focus. With 2x2 as a guiding framework, the following preparations will help you execute your efforts in a thorough and sustainable manner.

Prepare for the Paradigm Shift

Moving the DEI is a paradigm shift from exclusion to inclusion, and creating that kind of change is often a very difficult venture. Progress could require a high-level strategic paradigm shift, like rebranding, entering a new market, or offering a disruptive product or service.

Recognize that this is no easy or quick transformation. Yes, some elements can be implemented quickly, but the transformation will be more challenging depending on where the organization initially scored on the awareness and acceptance scales. Hiding behind those scores might be stubborn biases that are difficult to change. In some cases, those who are unwilling to move their individual DEI needle may need to exit the organization. This step is not to be taken lightly, but with the understanding that *everyone* must move their needle to the top right quadrant for an organization to make the paradigm shift from exclusion to inclusion,

Communicate

The first action step is assessing your awareness and your current action. Do the assessments and study the results. Then, before taking further action, hold listening sessions in groups and with individuals from all levels. Understand your workforce. Begin your pivot to inclusivity by understanding the perspective of every employee, whether through ERG groups or other existing constructs. This is the crux of an inclusive culture.

I recognize that a CEO of a multinational organization does not have the time to sit down and listen to each individual in a private conversation. However, every supervisor can listen to the five, ten, or even twenty people who directly report to them. Doing so is critical. Employees engage much more when they believe their supervisor, manager, or director authentically listens to them and appreciates their perspective. When every person in an oversight role authentically listens to their direct reports, the company will move the needle significantly and quickly.

Foster Innovative Flexibility

Change is fostered by flexibility in action and attitudes. By listening to everyone, leaders will hear diverse perspectives and ideas that vary widely in merit. Be flexible in your approach. Be willing to change as you become aware of potential problems and incredible opportunities.

Earlier, we discussed how certainty is the flipside of the awareness coin. Flexible mindset is the method by which we flip that coin and move the DEI needle.

Also be flexible in the programs you support. Remember, as a leader your goal is to make your people as successful as possible. That requires flexibility in decision-making. Make the best decision possible but be willing to change your mind if the measures show it is not working. Be committed to success and flexible in how you achieve that success. Being committed to diversity, equity, and inclusion makes the methods less important than the results.

Remember, you support DEI because it delivers the best ROI for the organization. Exclusion often ignores the best ideas; this is why small innovative organizations are capable of disrupting established markets. Imagine if those traditional organizations had been willing to listen to the innovative ideas generated by diverse thinking.

Some actions will be very difficult for many, perhaps even so difficult they are deemed impossible by some. Removing the politics behind programs is one such action. Some programs are sometimes the pet projects of certain leaders and they defend them as if their career depends upon them. Instead, the organization must be willing to shift in order to solve problems. That means reassessing programs periodically. If the program is working, support it. If the program needs more resources to succeed, find the resources. If the program is failing, revise it or remove it.

Of course, assessing the viability of the program depends upon giving the program ample time to succeed. Exclusionary individuals will dismiss inclusionary programs because of their biased view-points. Beware of that political agenda because it does not benefit the organization.

Listen for Ideas

In the process of listening, be on the lookout for ideas to expand your inclusiveness. In those listening sessions, you will find what previously excluded individuals need. It might be a simple conversation with a dedicated employee to facilitate change. Be prepared to hear how other companies have created diversity departments, held training, designed communication campaigns, and hosted other initiatives.

In anticipation of those conversations, do your research. Reach out to connections and search online to see what other companies have done. In the process, you are raising your awareness of DEI pro-grams that you can implement. Having that awareness fosters the discussion with your team and facilitates their feedback.

Conduct Inclusion Training Sessions

Begin with the executive team and expand to the managerial level before extending to the frontline employees. First, facilitate training that emphasizes awareness of little-known facts about diversity, equity, and inclusion. Then create awareness of uncon-scious bias. Be careful to create awareness concerning the ROI of effectively-executed DEI, and do so with the understanding that many will see DEI training as simply the latest organizational fad that won't last. Counter this exclusionary approach with facts (statistics, case studies, and global trends) that illustrate the principle. Remem-ber, the purpose of DEI training is to move the needle of productivity and profitability as well.

Bring awareness to the many demographic groups who suffer bias, unfairness, and exclusion. Help everyone in the training to hear the perspective of different ethnicities, religions, genders, generations, and economic backgrounds. Help everyone appreciate the per-spective of others in the organization.

That is not to say this is an easy or simple thing to do. Creating awareness of exclusive behaviors is a delicate process, and people often become defensive and feel threatened. Tailoring your language to the task at hand can help. Instead of following most traditional DEI programs, which stress "you didn't" or "you don't," shift the language to "We used to" and "We want to." The shift from "you" to "we" is inclusive language. Still, exercise wisdom and caution: too often, "we" has been used as a compliance-gaining strategy that lacks authenticity. The desire to create an inclusive culture must be authentic.

Reconstruct Teams

Analyze each team. Do they foster the inclusion of the best ideas by appreciating diverse perspectives? Is that diversity seen in the faces around the table? Is that diversity heard in brainstorming? Is that diversity appreciated in decision-making?

Once again, the ultimate goal of DEI is to move the needle for production and profitability. Leaders must value all human resources in the organization to move that needle.

Revisit Hiring Practices

Often there is an unconscious bias in hiring. Too often, people are hired based on external factors that give preference to one candidate coming from the right college, with the right background, who dresses the right way and has the right references. Beware of excluding candidates based on what you deem right or wrong. Instead, focus on the value of perspective that the individual brings to the position.

Promote Pay Equity

Nothing fosters exclusion more than unequal pay. When one person gets paid more for doing the exact same job with the same level of experience and delivers the same productivity as another employee, you can expect complaints. Still, favoritism that benefits the majority exists. This problem must be rectified quickly, or it will continue to simmer and eventually boil over. Stated simply, unfair compensation divides the best of organizations.

Therefore, establish pay equity. Be aware, however, that this is where it becomes challenging or even difficult to keep politics out of compensation. We all know that organizations are riddled with the politics of personal advancement and individual desires for power. We all want to get ahead, and too many of us are willing to go the extra mile to get what we want. As much as we may want to promote inclusion, the temptation to skew standards in our favor is intense. But however tempting, the truth is that inclusiveness requires pay and compensation equity. If everyone is of value, pay must be based on merit and compensated fairly. Any unfairness will erode the foundations of even the most successful organizations.

Assess Company Policies, Practices, and Procedures

The core values of any organization are reflected in its policies, practices, and procedures. Begin by analyzing your company policies because that is where practices and procedures are codified. Leaders consult the policy manual when any disagreement in practices or procedures arises. When creating awareness for DEI, leaders often need to revisit the policy manual to ensure that a) these policies are in step with their new awareness, and b) that the practices and procedures abide by the intent of the policies. Look for bias, whether intended or unintended.

Re-examining your policies, practices, and procedures brings bias to light. For example, what is your policy about celebrating holidays? Do you give employees Christmas off but make employees celebrating holidays of other religions use paid time off? DEI doesn't dictate that every employee gets every holiday off. Some organizations establish X number of holidays they will celebrate that year. Then they allow the employees to choose which holidays they will observe. That will not work for every organization, but a fair approach—whatever it looks like in practice—does.

Moving the needle for DEI and ultimate productivity and profitability requires assessing and reassessing policies, practices, and procedures periodically, often annually. Focus on fairness, not tradition or convenience. The policies need not be equal; as we discussed earlier, they must be equitable.

Track Progress

Many valuable initiatives never succeed, in part because accountability was never established.

Leaders are wise to track the progress of DEI initiatives by regularly measuring both awareness and acceptance. I suggest revising the questions and content for 2x2 assessment at least annually. Annual reviews, if conducted with integrity, provide an excellent way to increase awareness and monitor the acceptance of the individual employee.

Organizations are wise to monitor not only their demographics but also other attributes of awareness and acceptance. Are our numbers in the appropriate range? Are our approaches fostering inclusion? Where are we succeeding? Where do we need to focus our attention for improvement?

Facilitate Ongoing Feedback

To track progress effectively, constantly seek feedback. Do not wait for the annual review to do so. After all, the best time to fix a problem is when it occurs. Why wait? Ask yourself:

- Where are you on the 2x2 grid?
- Are you non inclusive?
- Are you willing but not curious?
- Are you curious but not yet willing to commit to inclusive action?

You can move the needle by changing your attitude or actions wherever you are on the grid. In the end, you will hopefully come to realize that DEI is a valuable way to transform your organization, maximize opportunities, and deliver peak profits. Diversity of perspectives drives innovation and employee engagement.

CONCLUSION

Moving the DEI needle from exclusion to inclusion requires moving from unaware to understanding; unwilling to willing. This challenging paradigm shift requires assessment, re-assessment, strategic action, flexibility, and accountability. This is a long journey. Unless the top leadership are already in the inclusion quadrant on the AxA framework, chances of progress within the organization are lower. Consider a concentric circle approach that starts at the top. This is a very important strategic item not only for the management but also for the board.

KEY TAKEAWAYS:

- Actions focused on awareness and acceptance will increase inclusion.
- Sustaining and reinforcing steady action will foster change.
- This is a transformation. It will take time, energy, and sacrifices.
- The journey is as important as the goal.

CHAPTER 10:

DO NOT GIVE UP

We must do it right, partly because we have done it wrong (at least to some extent) for so long. Diversity, equity, and inclusion are not simply the latest fad or compliance construct. Inclusion is recognizing, engaging, and appreciating the many different fabrics of life that make each of us unique and valuable. To continue to ignore or dismiss diversity is to be blind to beauty and poisoned against potential. Failing to appreciate diversity right is limiting our vision and potential.

We must wake up.

We must not give up.

We must do it right.

Diversity is Everywhere

Diversity exists in all things on this earth. It exists in our looks, ability, age, and sexual orientation. Diversity is also found in our language, geography, and priorities. Nature includes all forms of diversity and equally celebrates the mountains and the prairies, the polar ice caps, and the tropical beaches. We see the diversity in the snow and the sunshine, the floods and the droughts, fierce hurricane winds, and refreshing breezes. Look no farther than the seasons to find the diversity of the springtime blossoms, summer growth, fall harvest, and winter rest.

Pause to notice the diversity represented in world cultures. We often celebrate the same holiday in different ways. For example, European and North American cultures celebrate Christmas as the climatic winter holiday, while Australia celebrates it in the middle of summer. Within many religions, a variety of branches and sects interpret the same sacred documents differently. Each celebrates their faith and holiday traditions based on region, family tradition, and personal preference. Diversity is heard in many different languages and dialects. Even amongst birth families, we see the diversity of personalities. No two people are identical—not even identical twins.

Diversity is prevalent everywhere we look. Pause and notice the diversity around you. Then remember that to detail each of these differences would require a lengthy book.

Yet, we are tempted to make the world similar to avoid feelings of discomfort that can arise when we attempt to include those who are different in skin color, ethnicity, and language. At the same time, we subconsciously favor those with whom we share a common background, faith, and worldview. We also bias our actions regarding gender, in many cases based on our past experiences and pattern recognition. The very notion of welcoming a different perspective is harder than we often think. Too often, our teachings tell us to fight back against differences and push back against broken patterns. "Those people" are branded as aliens or foreigners. They are seen as "outsiders" and even "sinners" or "rebels" who threaten our organizational cohesiveness.

Even in our work with organizations, where the value of inclusiveness fosters creativity and innovation, "we" are often made uncomfortable by "them." As leaders, we demand obedience under the illusion that uniformity ensures the best productivity and profitability. Nothing could be further from the truth, especially within innovative organizations. Diversity and inclusion, not uniformity and exclusion, are the building blocks of creativity and innovation. That is the fertile soil from which new ideas grow and blossom.

We haven't done it all right because we often see diversity, equity, and inclusion as checking a box, being politically correct, or satisfying an external requirement. That is the wrong way to think about DEI. Instead, we need to understand how exclusion wastes valuable human resources, creates unnecessary division, and deflects the best opportunities. We haven't done it right, and we need to. If we don't, we will miss the best opportunities *and* our social responsibilities.

Diversity, equity, and inclusion are valuable methods for achieving the best success in any business, community organization, or culture.

We Are All Connected

We are no longer isolated islands in a vast world; we do not solely live our lives with our immediate family, in the neighborhood in which we grew up. Today we are all connected: across the globe and through a variety of avenues. Technology connects us as we log onto the web or interact through social media. Within business, multinational corporations that require international travel and working with diverse foreign and domestic teams are common.

Census numbers show a shrinking majority population and rising minority populations. This is reflected in political matters that will not simply be dismissed. The faces of our families are changing with increasing numbers of multi-racial couples and children. Our communities no longer look like they did in sitcoms from the 1950s. Migration has led to millions immigrating and creating multicultural societies from those that were monocultural just a few decades ago. Ultimately, our organizations and communities also reflect that change. They simply do not look like they did a few decades ago. Failing to admit that is to deny the facts.

Listen to the topics of conversation within our workplaces. Discussing DEI shows that it is real. How do we not discuss it when so many differences are evident? Why would we want to avoid DEI topics? We must do it right, and we must do it now. Diversity is one of the eternal realities of life and society.

Never Dismiss "Them"

Despite this reality, shifting from a mindset of exclusion to inclusion is very threatening to many. It is important to mitigate this difficulty by trying to understand those who are accustomed to unbroken patterns that create a safe, predictable, and comfortable world. Listen and feel their pain, remembering that they have worked their way through the organizational ranks, played by the rules, and now expect to enjoy their promised benefits. Imagine how they feel when the rules are changed suddenly, and the advantages they once held disappear.

Also understand the difficulty those in power sometimes experience when expected to share power with those that were once minimized, belittled, or excluded. Their unbroken patterns created an arrogance that is now being threatened, if not shattered. Some might claim, "It's about time. They deserve the pain they are getting." While that may be the case, dismissing anyone we label as "them" is exclusion.

Creating room for change often brings discomfort and resistance. We all want our chance and, if we are totally honest, want an advantage beyond merit. That is part of being a human. And it is why, as leaders, it is difficult to create room for DEI without hard work. Everyone in our personal and professional lives set their priorities and creates standards and metrics that justify our actions.

There you will find a snapshot of the situation and values. What are your DEI numbers? Based on those numbers, where do you fall on the 2x2 grid? What needs to change?

Keep Creating Opportunity

As valuable as metrics are, they are simply the first step. Please don't stop at that point, lest you be lulled into believing you are maximizing your opportunities. Equity is about creating equal opportunity, which then enables the opportunity for outcomes. Equity must become a core value in your organization because DEI has a powerful ROI that you are wise to follow.

Engage your own qualitative and quantitative assessments. Listen and watch for inequities that are not only denying individuals an opportunity for inclusion, participation, and engagement but for missed opportunities for the organization. Think beyond the department label of "Human Resources" and grasp the value that each employee offers. Are you wasting valuable resources? Would you accept that level of waste for raw manufacturing materials? Of course not.

Notice the challenges for those that have been overlooked or dismissed. For example, notice the wasted time and efforts of an individual physically challenged with steps, narrow doorways, or other physical obstacles. Notice the proximity to restrooms or other necessary facilities. Notice where you hold after-hours social gatherings. Also, notice the conversation. Who is excluded? What cost does that incur?

Now imagine that excluded person seeing the mission statement boldly painted on the wall claiming DEI as a core value. How can you expect any of those individuals to engage and deliver their peak productivity?

Instead, how can you create new opportunities where they are included, feel valued, and help create an innovative culture?

No Easy Choice

Inclusion is a choice, but not an easy one. The difficulty of that choice may mean some only feel safe engaging in intellectual tourism. They might be willing to learn but not curious enough to take action. Recognize that embracing DEI requires a conscious and strategic commitment, a willing sacrifice by those in power to share instead of hoard. That deliberate choice to include must be thoughtful. Like every other wise leadership and organizational decision, it must value the context and the outcome.

The choice also includes the speed of that change. Some will want immediate change, while others want no change at all. How fast can you change? How much can you change?

As leaders, we must remember that our current state results from human history. Significant paradigm shifts didn't happen in a moment but required conscious, consistent pressure. Even after the shift, considerable effort was required to sustain the change. There are always those unwilling to change that will work relentlessly to reverse it. Make a conscious choice to sustain the change.

We All Must Engage

My father was forced to migrate from the country now called Bangladesh to India due to political wars and the country's religious division. Overnight he lost his home, farm, and roots. He moved to a new country as a boy, dressed only in his shorts and partly unbuttoned shirts. There he was one of many in his uncle's crowded house in Kolkata. Nevertheless, he earned his accounting degree, raised a family, and integrated into India. His success was made possible, at least partially, because he felt included.

My immigration to North America several years back was much easier and welcoming. Even though I am a visible minority and will always stand out from the skin color of many around me, I am integrated into the society. I live, work, and give back to this place that I now call my home. I am grateful to all my friends and colleagues who make me feel at home.

But it wasn't just their action. I made a conscious choice to engage in my new world. I didn't sit back and wait for others to reach out to me; I made the decision to become part of the ecosystem. I could have claimed the identity of a foreigner and restricted myself within a certain immigrant community. I know a lot of folks of various immigrant communities who lived their whole life, connecting, partying, and socially interacting only within their respective communities. I'm glad I made the wise decision to reach out and choose to be included in the larger diverse community.

I learned a lot of new things and took an active interest in my adopted country. For example, I grew up watching cricket as a sport. I did not know anything about ice hockey. Then there was baseball. Why did they play without wickets? Now I love both sports very much. Besides on the television I am often at the live games and genuinely enjoy them.

This journey is not about majorities welcoming the minority. Instead, it is about where we are going and how quickly we can get there. Our journey requires that we all contribute and value the contribution.

Notice that this is a journey, not just a destination. As we travel through our lives, we have three choices. We can choose to live the life of a hermit, pretending we have all we need in isolation. Or we can choose to journey alone, complaining about "those people" who are different. We can choose to join others on a fascinating journey that takes us farther and to more exciting locations. This journey is filled with curiosity and willingness, creativity and innovation, camaraderie and exhilaration. Ultimately, the best journey moves the needle, engaging us to live our best lives and accomplish far more than we ever imagined.

Which journey do you choose?

Equity is Possible

Despite difficulties along the way, our destination is not out of reach. If we are willing to join the journey, we will find that we are not seeking a utopia of equality. We know that is not possible. Yet equity is.

It is happening today in the world of business. Progress being made; committed leaders have moved the needle of DEI. That is encouraging. Many corporations are multi-national and reflect diversity on their boards and in their workforce. Also, notice the powerful influence of those corporations. Their influence often leads entire cultures on the DEI journey.

Moving the needle requires a concerted effort in the present and over time. We must be diligent in our efforts, often only taking baby steps on our journey but willing to take giant leaps at others. We must never be content where we are and stop short of our destination. Instead, we must forge ahead.

But if we do not focus on holistic awareness of the dimensions, adopt equity as a principle, and commit to the journey towards inclusion, changes will be temporary and will revert back to the current state with the change of regime and circumstances.

Remember, this isn't simply the minority complaining about the majority. This is about appreciating the diversity available, the value of resting on equity, and including everyone on the journey. The journey isn't a win-lose debate but rather a collaborative effort to solve significant problems. Our focus on DEI isn't merely a social tactic to shift power but rather a new paradigm for living peacefully and working productively.

KEY TAKEAWAYS:

- The journey we choose is our choice.
- We can choose our destination and companions.
- Be prepared. The journey requires consistent progress and will take time.
- We cannot ever give up on the journey.
- Our commitment must be to make the world better for the next generation, not just better for an investor call scheduled in the upcoming quarter.

ACKNOWLEDGEMENTS

I acknowledge all my readers who took the time to read my first book, *Leadership 4.0*. Your encouragement gave me the courage to write *Let's Do it Right* and discuss a sensitive topic like DEI.

I acknowledge my wife, who puts up with my numerous hobbies and passions.

I am thankful to all the fantastic, more talented authors who presented the gift of knowledge through their work and helped enrich me.

Finally, I thank my team, who are the most amazing professionals and humans I have ever worked with.

REFERENCES

Accenture.com (Getting to Equal: The Disability Inclusion Advantage, Accenture https://www.accenture.com/_acnmDEIa/pdf-89/accenture-disability-inclusion-research-report.pdf)

Adams, James Truslow. "Lesson Plan: The American Dream." 1931. Library of Congress. Retrieved October 30, 2020.

American Development Index http://www.measureofamerica.org/10yearsandcounting/

American Psychological Association, 2014. https://www.apa.org/topics/neuropsychology/men-women-cognitive-skills

Astell, Mary. *Some Reflections on Marriage*. 1700.

Axios.com. https://www.axios.com/2022/09/07/approval-of-interracial-marriage-america

Biography.com. https://www.biography.com/scientist/franz-boas.

Boeing.com. https://www.boeing.com/principles/diversity-and-inclusion/annual-report/our-stories.page.

Boston.com. *News*. http://archive.boston.com/news/education/higher/articles/2005/01/17/summers_remarks_on_women_draw_fire/?__goto=loginpage

Brady, K. "Methods of Diminishing Total Survey Error by Eliminating Bias." *Quirk's Media*. February 1, 2016. https://www.quirks.com/articles/methods-of-diminishing-total-survey-error-by-eliminating-bias

Bureau of Labor Statistics Reports, April 21, 2021. https://www.bls.gov/news.release/archives/empsit_05072021.pdf

Catalyst.org. "Women in the Workforce: United States (Quick Take)." Oct 14, 2020.

Chamorro-Premuzic, Thomas "Does Diversity Actually Increase Creativity?" *Harvard Business Review*. June 28, 2017. https://hbr. org/2017/06/does-diversity-actually-increase-creativity

Columbia Law School. (https://www.law.columbia.edu/news/archive/ kimberle-crenshaw-intersectionality-more-two-decades-later)

Cort, John C. "Christian Socialism." Orbis Books, New York, 1988. pp. 355.

Cuncic, Arlin. "The Psychology of Racism" February 02, 2022https://www. verywellmind.com/the-psychology-of-racism-

DailyHisotry.org https://dailyhistory.org/ Are_there_Ancient_Roots_to_Socialism

Darwin, C., On the Origin of Species, 1859.

Deloitte (Deloitte Review, Jan 2018 https://www2.deloitte.com/ content/dam/insights/us/articles/4209_Diversity-and -inclusion-revolution/DI_Diversity-and-inclusion-revolution.pdf)

Diamond, Jared. *Guns, Germs, and Steel*.

Diversity Inc. https://www.diversityinc.com/diversityinc-top-50-2022/

Eagly, Alice. *Sex Differences in Social Behavior: A Social-Role Interpretation* (1987, Lawrence Erlbaum; 1st edition).

Equal Employment Opportunity Commission

Diversity in High Tech https://www.eeoc.gov/special-report/ diversity-high-tech

(Sonja Sepahban, Aug 4, 2022, Our Office.com https://www.ouroffice. io/2020/08/04/the-new-roi-return-on-inclusion/)

The Folly of Fools: The Logic of Deceit and Self-Deception in Human Life, Basic Books, 2011.

Foxbusiness.com, June 2, 2020

Galton, F. *Hereditary Genius*. 1869

Gartner.com (Top Ten Technologies Driving the Digital Workplace. https://www.gartner.com/smarterwithgartner/ top-10-technologies-driving-the-digital-workplace)

Gollwitzer, A. and John Bargh. "Why are people prejudiced? The answer is not what you think." Published 1:53 PM EST, Mon

January 29, 2018. https://www.cnn.com/2018/01/29/opinions/
prejudice-broken-patterns-opinion-gollwitzer-bargh).

Harvard Business Review. "How to Measure Inclusion in the Workplace,"
by Lauren Romansky, Mia Garrod, Katie Brown, and Kartik Deo, May
27, 2021. https://hbr.org/2021/05/how-to-measure-inclusion-in-th
e-workplace.

Henderson, William L, Larry C Ledebur, "Government Incentives and
Black Economic Development." Denison University.

History.com. https://www.history.com/news/
humans-evolution-neanderthals-denisovans

Hutchison, J. *Psychological Safety and Transparent Communication
at Work: Strengthening Collaboration and Innovation* [Video].
April 8, 2020.

Ingram, P. "The Forgotten Dimension of Diversity: Social Class is as
Important as Race or Gender." *Harvard Business Review.* January–
February 2021.

International Women's Day 2022 IWD 2022#BREAKTHEBIAS.

Kaimenyi from Nairobi and Senaji. "Influence of political environment
on the implementation of workforce diversity policies in public
universities in Kenya" by Catherine K. Kaimenyi, Faculty of Business
Studies, Chuka University, Prof. Harriet J. Kidombo, School of
Continuing and Distance Education, University of Nairobi and Dr.
Thomas Senaji School of Business and Economics, Kenya Methodist
University.

LearningEnglish.com. https://learningenglish.voanews.com/a/
gay-marriage-up-70-in-us-since-legalization/5593232.html0

Leonardelli, Geoffrey J. and Marilynn B. Brewer. "Minority and Majority
Discrimination: When and Why." *Journal of Experimental Social
Psychology* 37, 468–485. (2001)doi:10.1006/jesp.2001.1475, available
online at http://www.idealibrary.com.

Lewontin, R. and Stephen Jay Gould, "The Spandrels of San Marco
and the Panglossian Paradigm: A Critique of the Adaptationist
Programme." Proceedings of the Royal Society of London. Series B,
Biological Sciences, Vol. 205, No.1161, *The Evolution of Adaptation
by Natural Selection*, pp. 581-598. Sep. 21, 1979. Accessed in http://
ecoevo.wdfiles.com/local—files/start/GouldLewontin1979.pdf)

Lewontin, R. (1972) "The Apportionment of Human Diversity."

Mahin, Stephanie, Ph.D., and Shoshana Rosenberg, J.D., MBA, FIP, PLS, CIPP, CIPM. https://kenaninstitute. unc.edu/wp-content/uploads/2021/02/ KenanInsights-OrganizationalEquity-02232021-r.pdf

Marquet, David. *Turn the Ship Around*. 2021.

McKinsey.com https://www.mckinsey.com/featured-insights/ diversity-and-inclusion/how-the-lgbtq-plus-community-fare s-in-the-workplace

McKinsey.com The Future of Diversity, Equity, and Inclusion 2022 https://www.affirmity.com/future-diversity-equity-inclusion-2022- (https://www.mckinsey.com/~/media/mckinsey/ featured%20insights/diversity%20and%20inclusion/ diversity%20wins%20how%20inclusion%20matters/ diversity-wins-how-inclusion-matters-vf.pdf)

Modern Parenthood, November 4, 2015.

Murray, C. Human Diversity: The Biology of Gender, Race, and Class (2020)

Murray, C., and Richard J. Herrnstein (1994) "The Bell Curve"

Mitchell, Bruce (HOLC "Redlining" Maps: The Persistent Structure Of Segregation And Economic Inequality, By Bruce Mitchell PhD., Senior Research Analyst and Juan Franco, Senior GIS Specialist, NCRC / March 20, 2018 / https://ncrc.org/holc/)

Patten, Eileen. "Roles of Moms and Dads Converge as They Balance Work and Family." March 14, 2013

MyCareersFuture.com "Pros & Cons of a Multi-Generational Workforce" https://content.mycareersfuture.gov.sg/ pros-cons-of-a-multi-generational-workforce)

New York Times https://www.nytimes.com/2006/02/22/ education/22harvard.html

NCRC.org "HOLC 'Redlining' Maps: The Persistent Structure Of Segregation And Economic Inequality." By Bruce Mitchell PhD., Senior Research Analyst and Juan Franco, Senior GIS Specialist, NCRC / March 20, 2018 / https://ncrc.org/holc/)

Oh, Jean. "Mapping the Class Ceiling: The Social Class Disadvantage for Attaining Management Positions." *Academy of Management Discoveries* Vol. 8, No. 1. March 2022.

PBS.org https://www.pbs.org/fmc/interviews/wilson.htm)

Pew Research Center. December 17, 2015. *Parenting in America* (February 4, 2016). "Most Americans Say Government Doesn't Do Enough to Help Middle Class."

Https://www.pewresearch.org/fact-tank/2022/04/20/how-the-american-middle-class-has-changed-in-the-past-five-decades/

Posner, Cydney. Caproate Governance. June 9, 2021.

Quiroz-Gutierrez, Marco. *Fortune.* May 6, 2021.

Rae, Douglas et al. (eds.). *Equalities.* Cambridge: Harvard University Press, 1981.

Raj, Suhasini, "India's Next President Will Make History When She's Sworn In." July 21, 2022. https://www.nytimes.com/2022/07/21/world/asia/india-president.html

Randstad.com (https://www.randstad.com.sg/about-us/press-releases/singapore-employees-prefer-same-age-or-older-managers/)

Randstad.com (https://www.randstad.com.sg/about-us/press-releases/singapore-employees-prefer-same-age-or-older-managers/

Rawls, J. 1971, p. 21 f. Rawls [A Theory of Justice. Harvard University Press, Cambridge, MA, 1971].

PricewaterhouseCoopers (https://www.pwc.com/gx/en/about/diversity/internationalwomensday/the-female-millennial.html)

Ricardo, David. *Principles of Political Economy and Taxation.* 1817.

Romansky, L, Mia Garrod, Katie Brown and Kartik Deo. "How to Measure Inclusion in the Workplace." *Harvard Business Review.* May 27, 2021. https://hbr.org/2021/05/how-to-measure-inclusion-in-the-workplace.)

Ryan, Alan. *On Politics.* Book II. 2012. pp. 647–651.

Sepahban, Sonja. Aug 4, 2022. Our Office.com https://www.ouroffice.io/2020/08/04/the-new-roi-return-on-inclusion/)

Starbucks. October 14, 2020, in Stories.com. https: /stories.starbucks. com, June 12, 2021

Swarthmore.edu (https://www.swarthmore.edu/bulletin/archive/wp/ january-2009_what-larry-summers-said-and-didnt-say.html)

Temkin, Larry S. Aggregation within lives: Social Philosophy and Policy 26 (1):1-29 (2009)

Temkin, Larry S. "Inequality, Philosophy, and Public Affairs." 15 (2):99-121 (1986)

Temkin, Larry S. Inequality. Oxford University Press, 1993.

Trivers, R. The Folly of Fools: The Logic of Deceit and Self-Deception in Human Life. Basic Books, 2011.

Twitter.com (https://twitter.com/RealAbril/ status/1341135824730013696?s=20)

Wired.com. June 2021. https://www.wired.com/story/ google-timnit-gebru-ai-what-really-happened/

Twitter (https://twitter.com/RealAbril/ status/1341135824730013696?s=20)

University of Cambridge https://www.equality.admin.cam.ac.uk/ equality-and-diversity-cambridge/

Wall Street Journal.com, June 12, 2020.

Wang, W. and Kim Parker. "Record Share of Americans Have Never Married, As Values, Economics and Gender Patterns Change." September 24, 2014.

Weforum.com "Getting to Equal: the Disability Inclusion Advantage." Accenture https://www.accenture.com/_acnmedia/pdf-89/ accenture-disability-inclusion-research-report.pdf) (What companies gain by including persons with disabilities Apr 23, 2019. https://www.weforum.org/agenda/2019/04/ what-companies-gain-including-persons-disabilities-inclusion/ https://www.weforum.org/agenda/2019/04/what-companies -gain-including-persons-disabilities-inclusion/)

Westen 1990, p. 10. Speaking of Equality: An Analysis of the Rhetorical Force of 'Equality' in Moral and Legal Discourse. pp. 257-284. Princeton University Press, 1990.

Wikipedia.com (https://en.wikipedia.org/wiki/Racism_in_Asia) and Africa (https://en.wikipedia.org/wiki/Racism_in_Africa

Wired.com https://www.wired.com/story/
google-timnit-gebru-ai-what-really-happened/

Witten, Sarah. CNBC, April 17, 2018. https://www.cnbc.
com/2018/04/17/starbucks-to-close-all-stores-o
n-may-29-for-racial-bias-education-day.html#:~:text=Starbucks%20
said%20Tuesday%20it%20will,at%20a%20Starbucks%20in%20
Philadelphia.)

World Economic Forum. "What Companies Gain by Including Persons
With Disabilities." Apr 23, 2019.

Yale News, Sept 12, 2012, https://news.yale.edu/2012/09/24/
scientists-not-immune-gender-bias-yale-study-shows

YouTube
https://www.youtube.com/watch?v=I8F7GZnERNU
https://www.youtube.com/watch?v=92PiMSa_kCY
https://www.youtube.com/watch?v=FOUmhUr0SSk

USAtoday.com. June 11, 2020.

U.S. Bureau of Labor Reports, April 21, 2021.

U.S. Census Bureau https://www.census.gov/library/publications/2021/
acs/acsbr-009.html

ABOUT THE

AUTHOR

Debasis "DB" Bhaumik is an entrepreneurial leader who has worked with and for many global Fortune 100 organizations across Asia-Pacific, Europe, and North America. He started his career as a technology entrepreneur in India and has carried out various roles in technology leadership in North America. He is a well-respected senior leader and Board Member. DB is also the author of Amazon #1 Best seller *Leadership 4.0*, which is based on the belief that "Technology is a commodity; people are the differentiators."

www.ingramcontent.com/pod-product-compliance
Lightning Source LLC
Chambersburg PA
CBHW030512210326
41597CB00013B/881